Tolley's
Stamp Duties
and
Stamp Duty Reserve Tax

4th Edition

by
Patrick Cannon LLB BCL ATII *Solicitor*

Tolley Publishing Company Limited

un A United News & Media publication

Published by
Tolley Publishing Company Ltd
Tolley House
2 Addiscombe Road
Croydon, Surrey CR9 5AF England
0181–686 9141

Photoset by
Phoenix Photosetting, Chatham, Kent

Printed and bound in Great Britain by
Hobbs the Printers, Southampton

About this Book

This book is written for busy practitioners seeking a brief, concise guide to the stamp duties and the stamp duty reserve tax. This edition is up to date as of 31 May 1995 and includes the relevant provisions of the Finance Act 1995.

The chapters are in alphabetical order of subject for quick reference and there is a detailed index, tables of cases, statutes and statutory instruments.

Patrick Cannon is a solicitor and a member of the Chartered Institute of Taxation.

Comments on this book and suggestions for improvements are welcome.

TOLLEY PUBLISHING CO. LTD.

Contents

Contents

Abbreviations and References

ABBREVIATIONS

A-G	=	Attorney-General.
CA	=	Court of Appeal.
CCR	=	Court for Crown Cases Reserved (roughly equivalent in status to the Court of Appeal).
Cf.	=	Compare.
Ch D	=	Chancery Division.
CIR	=	Commissioners of Inland Revenue.
CP	=	Common Pleas Division (now part of the Queen's Bench Division).
CP (I)	=	Common Pleas Division (Ireland).
CS	=	Court of Session (Scotland).
Ex D	=	Exchequer Division (now part of the Chancery Division).
Ex (S)	=	Court of Exchequer (Scotland).
FA	=	Finance Act.
FSA	=	Financial Services Act.
HL	=	House of Lords.
ICTA	=	Income and Corporation Taxes Act 1988.
KB	=	King's Bench Division.
PC	=	Privy Council.
PDA	=	Probate, Divorce and Admiralty Division (now Family Division).
QB	=	Queen's Bench Division.
s	=	Section.
SA	=	Stamp Act 1891.
Sch	=	Schedule.
SDMA	=	Stamp Duties Management Act 1891.
SI	=	Statutory Instrument.
SR & O	=	Statutory Rules and Orders.
TCGA	=	Taxation of Chargeable Gains Act 1992.

REFERENCES (*denotes current series)

AC	=	*Law Reports, Appeal Cases, (Incorporated Council of Law Reporting for England and Wales, 3 Stone Buildings, Lincoln's Inn, London WC2A 3XN).
Ad & E	=	Adolphus & Ellis's Reports.
All ER	=	*All England Law Reports, (Butterworth & Co. (Publishers) Ltd., 88 Kingsway, London WC2B 6AB).
App Cas	=	Law Reports, Appeal Cases.
ATC	=	Annotated Tax Cases, (Gee & Co. (Publishers) Ltd., 7 Swallow Place, London W1R 8AB).
B & Ad	=	Barnewall & Adolphus's Reports.

Abbreviations and References

B & Ald	=	Barnewall & Alderson's Reports.
B & C	=	Barnewall & Cresswall's Reports.
B & S	=	Best & Smith's Reports.
BTC	=	*British Tax Cases.
CB	=	Common Bench Reports.
Ch	=	*Law Reports, Chancery Division.
Ch App	=	Law Reports, Chancery Appeals.
CM & R	=	Crompton, Meeson & Roscoe's Reports.
E & B	=	Ellis & Blackburn's Reports.
East	=	East's Reports.
Ex D	=	Law Reports, Exchequer Division.
Exch	=	Exchequer Reports.
F(Ct of Sess)	=	Fraser, Court of Session Cases, 5th Series.
HL Cas	=	Clark's House of Lords Cases.
IR	=	*Irish Reports, (Law Reporting Council, Law Library, Four Courts, Dublin).
Ir LR	=	Irish Law Reports.
KB	=	Law Reports, King's Bench Division.
LR	=	Law Reports (followed by Court abbreviation).
LT	=	Law Times Reports.
M & W	=	Meeson & Welsby's Reports.
P	=	Law Reports, Probate, Divorce & Admiralty Division.
QB/QBD	=	*Law Reports, Queen's Bench Division.
QBR	=	Queen's Bench Reports.
R (Ct of Sess)	=	Rettie, Court of Session Cases, 4th Series.
SC	=	*Court of Session Cases (Scotland).
Sc LR	=	Scottish Law Reporter.
SLT	=	Scots Law Times Reports.
Sol Jo	=	Solicitors' Journal, Oyez Publishing Ltd, Norwich House, 11/13 Norwich St, London EC4A 1AB.
STC	=	*Simon's Tax Cases, (Butterworth & Co. (Publishers) Ltd., as above).
Taunt	=	Taunton's Reports.
TC	=	*Official Tax Cases, (H.M. Stationery Office, P.O. Box 276, London SW8 5DT).
TLR	=	Times Law Reports.
WLR	=	*Weekly Law Reports, (Incorporated Council of Law Reporting, as above).
WN	=	Weekly Notes, (Incorporated Council of Law Reporting, as above).

The first number in the citation refers to the volume, and the second to the page, so that [1978] 2 WLR 10 means that the report is to be found on page ten of the second volume of the Weekly Law Reports for 1978. Where no volume number is given, only one volume was produced in that year. Some series, such as the ATC, have continuous volume numbers. Where legal decisions are very recent and in the lower Courts, it must be remembered that they may be reversed on appeal. But references to the official Tax Cases ('TC') may be taken as final.

In English cases, Scottish and N. Irish decisions (unless there is a difference of law between the countries) are generally followed but are not binding, and Republic of Ireland decisions are considered (and vice versa). Privy Council decisions are of persuasive, but not binding, authority.

Acts of Parliament and Statutory Instruments (SI) (formerly Statutory Rules and Orders) (SR & O) are obtainable from H.M. Stationery Office (bookshop at 49 High Holborn, London WC1V 6HB; orders to P.O. Box 276, London SW8 5DT). Telephone orders should be made to 0171–873 9090, general enquiries to 0171–873 0011.

Table of Cases

Where the CIR are a party, the case is indexed only under the name of the taxpayer

Table of Cases

Table of Cases

Table of Cases

Table of Cases

Table of Statutes

Stamp Act 1891 1 Sch contains the heads of charge.

Table of Statutes

Table of Statutes

Table of Statutes

Table of Statutes

Table of Statutory Instruments

1 Introduction

1.1 Stamp duties have been charged since the *Stamp Act 1694*. There have been consolidating Acts. The last consolidating Acts are the *Stamp Act 1891* and the *Stamp Duties Management Act 1891*. These Acts remain the principal Acts but they have been amended by subsequent Finance Acts. The scheme of stamp duties has in general been simplified over the years. Following the abolition of CAPITAL DUTY (18) and unit trust instrument duty by *FA 1988*, the prospective abolition of stamp duty on transfers of shares and securities, bearer instrument duty and STAMP DUTY RESERVE TAX (73) was announced by *FA 1990*. The 1990 Budget Press Release stated that abolition would occur late in 1991/92 to coincide so far as possible with the introduction of paperless share dealing under the Stock Exchange's new share transfer system (TAURUS). Also linked to the introduction of TAURUS was the prospective abolition of stamp duty on property other than land and buildings provided for by *FA 1991*. However, on 11 March 1993, the Stock Exchange announced the indefinite suspension of development of TAURUS because of the complexity of the computer software. The project was taken over by a task force backed by the Bank of England, which announced in July 1993 the adoption of a slimmed-down electronic system known as 'CREST' to speed up the settlement of equity share trading in the London Stock Market. The new system is expected to be operational in 1996 and will provide a transfer mechanism for equity trades allowing those holding stock within the system to electronically receive stock and make payment. Unlike TAURUS, membership of CREST will be optional but those wishing to join will have to meet specific criteria. In a newsletter circulated to stockbrokers in early 1995 the CREST working party stated that the Inland Revenue was intending to seek statutory authority for making CREST calculate and collect stamp duty. It is therefore doubtful whether the abolition of stamp duty and STAMP DUTY RESERVE TAX (73) as announced by *FA 1990* and *FA 1991* will now occur.

The recent trend towards simplification of stamp duties was reversed by *FA 1994*. In particular, ad valorem conveyance on sale duty has been extended to the transfer of an interest in land or the grant of a lease in exchange for any property with the Government issuing official guidance on how to avoid an unintended double charge to sale duty: see 25.8 CONSIDERATION. Also in relation to transactions involving land, where the consideration cannot be ascertained it is now to be taken to be the market value of the land concerned and stamp duty charged accordingly instead of the fixed 50p duty which previously applied: see 25.9 CONSIDERATION. These changes fundamentally alter the structure of stamp duties in relation to land and unfortunately were not properly thought through before implementation and are still causing considerable uncertainty as to their scope and relationship with pre-existing stamp duty principles.

The following paragraphs summarise the structure of stamp duty law.

1.2   Introduction

1.2   **Stamp duties are charged on instruments** falling within specified heads of charge. [*SA, s 1*]. See 49 INSTRUMENTS and 20 CHARGEABILITY. Transactions which are carried out orally do not attract stamp duty; see 59 ORAL TRANS-ACTIONS for examples of transactions which may be carried out so as to avoid stamp duty. The enforcement of stamp duties is ensured by the conse-quences of FAILURE TO STAMP (41), which are the incidence of PENALTIES AND OFFENCES (64) and inadmissibility of the instruments in EVIDENCE (36). These consequences apply where an instrument has been insufficiently or incor-rectly stamped. There is a presumption in favour of the taxpayer that an instrument is properly stamped in the absence of contrary evidence. In relation to sales of securities STAMP DUTY RESERVE TAX (73) imposes a directly enforceable charge equivalent to the rate of stamp duty where an agreement to sell securities is not followed by the creation of a duly stamped instrument of transfer, transferring the securities to the purchaser.

1.3   For an instrument to be chargeable it must fall within one of the heads of charge in *SA, 1 Sch* and subsequent legislation. The head of charge is determined by the substance of the transaction recorded in an instrument rather than its form and the wording used by the parties is not conclusive. The tide of judicial opinion appears to be running against the tone of the judgment of Rowlatt J in *Cape Brandy Syndicate v IRC, [1921] 1 KB 64*: 'In a taxing Act one has to look merely at what is clearly said. There is no room for an intendment. There is no equity about a tax. There is no presumption about a tax. Nothing is to be read in, nothing is to be implied. One can only look fairly at the language used.' Compare that with the situation in *Fitch Lovell Ltd v CIR Ch D, [1962] 3 All ER 685* which concerned 'a scheme for the avoidance of, or at any rate a substantial reduction of, the stamp duty payable on a take-over bid into which, to use the words of the appellant company's solicitors, a little ingenuity has been put' per Wilberforce J. The appellant's case was dismissed. Part of Wilberforce's judgment reads, 'It seems to me that an analysis of this transaction which seeks to produce the result that the property re-sold is the same property as that first sold, if it can be made at all, involves a degree of formalism which the law in the applica-tion of s 58(4) should not indorse.' Vinelott J went further in his judgment in *Ingram v CIR Ch D, [1985] STC 835* where after stating that the transactions involved were highly artificial and considering the observations of Lord Atkin in *IRC v Duke of Westminster, [1936] AC 1* stated, 'Stamp Duty is a tax on instruments. But (in the language of the older cases) to determine whether an instrument falls within a chargeable category and the duty payable the court must ascertain the substance of the transaction effected by it.'

See 8 ANTI-AVOIDANCE.

If an instrument falls within two heads of charge, the Crown can only levy one duty, but may choose the higher (*Speyer Bros v CIR HL, [1908] AC 92*).

The principles of construction of a taxing statute apply, inter alia, as follows:

(*a*) the onus of proof is on the Crown to show that an instrument is within a stamp duty charge;

(*b*) the wording of a charge to stamp duty must be clear and unambiguous and if the language is clear, the court must give effect to it;

(*c*) in a case of real ambiguity, the construction most favourable to the taxpayer should be given.

There are numerous exemptions from specific heads of charge or from stamp duties generally (see 39 EXEMPT INSTRUMENTS). Here the onus is on the taxpayer to show that the instrument qualifies for exemption.

1.4 **Rates of duty** are prescribed for each head of charge and fall into two categories:

(*a*) **fixed duties** which comprise fixed sums payable on certain instruments; and

(*b*) **ad valorem duties** calculated by reference to value, usually the value of the consideration recorded in the instrument.

For summaries of the rates of duties see 4 AD VALOREM DUTIES and 43 FIXED DUTIES.

1.5 **Payment of duty** is generally to be made before or shortly after EXECUTION (38) of the instrument charged and there are penalties for late stamping. See 63 PAYMENT OF DUTY OR TAX and 64 PENALTIES AND OFFENCES. There is no general rule as to the incidence of duty but see 63 PAYMENT OF DUTY OR TAX for persons who have an obligation to ensure correct stamping.

1.6 The stamp duty legislation applies to GB (England, Wales and Scotland), though there are some special provisions for the purposes of Scots law—see 70 SCOTLAND. Separate charging provisions apply to Northern Ireland (which together with GB comprises the UK)—see 51 IRELAND. The stamp duty legislation does not apply in the Channel Islands or the Isle of Man.

1.7 **Administration** of stamp duties is carried out by the Commissioners of Inland Revenue (CIR) also referred to as 'the Board'. See 3 ADMINISTRA-TION.

2   Adjudication

2.1 Adjudication is the process whereby the Commissioners formally assess the amount of duty, if any, chargeable on an instrument. It is also a necessary step in the appeal procedure (see 9 APPEALS). Adjudication is normally conclusive of the liability of an instrument to stamp duty (see 2.5 below).

2.2 Adjudication

2.2 Adjudication may be

(*a*) voluntary (see 2.3 below) so as to ensure the correctness of stamp or to initiate an appeal to the High Court; or

(*b*) compulsory (see 2.4 below) where legislation or practice requires an assurance that the correct amount of duty has been paid, where an exemption has been claimed or where the correct basis of charging duty may not be clear.

2.3 VOLUNTARY [*SA, s 12*]

Any person may request the Commissioners to express their opinion with reference to any executed instrument on

(*a*) whether it is chargeable to duty;

(*b*) the amount of duty chargeable.

The procedure is straightforward. Currently, in England and Wales, the instrument and a certified copy of it are posted to The Stamp Office, Adjudication Customer Services Unit, Ridgeworth House, Liverpool Gardens, Worthing, West Sussex BN11 1XP. However, as a result of reorganisation it is expected that the four local offices listed in 3.5 ADMINISTRATION will offer an adjudication service towards the end of 1995. In addition to the instrument and certified copy, there must be a full disclosure of all the facts and circumstances affecting liability to duty. Failure to do so renders the offender liable to a fine of £25 [*SA, s 5*]—see 64 PENALTIES AND OFFENCES. Representations about liability and the amount of the duty may be included.

The Commissioners will not consider draft or partly executed instruments.

If no duty is chargeable, the instrument will be stamped 'Adjudged not chargeable with any stamp duty'.

If duty is chargeable, the Commissioners assess the duty and when the instrument is stamped in accordance with the assessment it is also stamped 'Adjudged duly stamped'.

The Commissioners may call for whatever information they think necessary to make an assessment (*R v CIR ex p. Evill KB, [1951] 2 TLR 857*).

2.4 COMPULSORY

The following are the principal cases where legislation provides that an adjudication stamp is obligatory.

(*a*) Where exemption is claimed from stamp duty on COMPANY REORGANISATIONS (23) under *FA 1986, ss 75, 76, 77*.

(*b*) Where exemption is claimed on transactions between ASSOCIATED COMPANIES (12) under *FA 1930, s 42*.

(*c*) Where exemption is claimed on conveyances, transfers or lettings to CHARITIES (21) under *FA 1982, s 129*.

(*d*) Conveyances in contemplation of sale chargeable under *FA 1965, s 90* (see 28 CONVEYANCE OR TRANSFER).

(*e*) Where exemption is claimed in respect of maintenance funds for historic buildings under *FA 1980, s 98* (see 75 TRUSTS AND TRUSTEES).

(*f*) Where the consideration for sale as calculated under *SA, s 57* is reduced to the value of the property conveyed under *FA 1980, s 102* (see 25 CONSIDERATION).

(*g*) Orders made by the court under the *Companies Act 1985, s 427*. In these cases the solicitors are required to give an undertaking to the court that the order will be submitted for adjudication.

These documents are not duly stamped unless they have been adjudicated and bear a stamp denoting that no duty is chargeable or that they are adjudged duly stamped.

2.5   Adjudication is not conclusive in the following cases.

(*a*) On a conveyance on sale of freehold land or a lease or agreement for lease for seven years or more—A PRODUCED STAMP (66) is also required. In practice adjudication and production may be effected at the same time. [*FA 1931, s 28*].

(*b*) Where an instrument is liable to more than one stamp [*SA, s 4*] adjudication of one stamp is not conclusive of the other. (See *Fitch Lovell Ltd v CIR Ch D, [1962] 3 All ER 685*.)

(*c*) BEARER INSTRUMENTS (13) on which duty is payable on issue must also bear the DENOTING STAMP (33) required by *FA 1963, s 60(3)*.

(*d*) Where an adjudication stamp was obtained by misrepresentation or non-disclosure of the relevant facts.

2.6   An applicant for adjudication is entitled to withdraw from the procedure at any time and to have his document returned to him. See also 58 NEGOTIATING WITH THE STAMP OFFICE.

3   Administration

3.1   The care and management of stamp duties is with the Commissioners of Inland Revenue. [*SDMA, s 1*].

3.2   Stamp duties in England and Wales are administered by the Controller of Stamps at

3.3   Administration

London Stamp Office
Bush House
South West Wing
Strand
London WC2B 4QN
Tel: 0171–438 7452/7314/7475

3.3   ADJUDICATION (2) matters are currently dealt with at

Worthing Stamp Office
Adjudication Customer Services Unit
Ridgeworth House
Liverpool Gardens
Worthing
West Sussex BN11 1XP
Tel: 01903 288899

(During 1995 it is expected that the four local offices in 3.5 below will
begin offering an adjudication service.)

3.4   A counter service in London is available at
Ground Floor
Bush House
South West Wing
Strand
London WC2B 4QN

The City Stamp Office at 61 Moorgate, London EC2 has closed.

3.5   There are also the following regional offices

Birmingham Stamp Office
Ground Floor
City House
140–146 Edmund Street
Birmingham B3 2JG
Tel: 0121–200 2616

Bristol Stamp Office
First Floor
The Pithay
All Saints Street
Bristol BS1 2NY
Tel: 0117–945 6874/75

Manchester Stamp Office
Alexandra House
14–42 The Parsonage
Manchester M60 9BT
Tel: 0161–833 0413

Newcastle Stamp Office
Aidan House
All Saints Office Centre
Newcastle-upon-Tyne NE1 2BG
Tel: 0191–261 1991

3.6   Stamp duties in Scotland are administered by

The Stamp Office (Scotland)
Mulbery House
16 Picardy Place
Edinburgh EH1 3NF
Tel: 0131–556 8511

3.7   Stamp duties in Northern Ireland are administered by the Commissioners of Inland Revenue through

Belfast Stamp Office
Ground Floor
Dorchester House
52–58 Great Victoria Street
Belfast BT2 7QE
Tel: 01232–314614

3.8   STAMP DUTY RESERVE TAX (73) is administered by a separate unit at the Worthing Stamp Office. Regional stamp offices do not deal with this tax. In Scotland general enquiries may be sent to the address in 3.6 above. However, all payments and notifications should be sent to the

SDRT Unit
Worthing Stamp Office
Ridgeworth House
Liverpool Gardens
Worthing
West Sussex BN11 1XP
Tel: 01903 288979

4   Ad Valorem Duties

4.1   Certain stamp duties are ad valorem, that is they are calculated by reference to the value of the transaction. For duties which are not ad valorem see 43 FIXED DUTIES.

The value on which the ad valorem duty is charged is sometimes the stated CONSIDERATION (25) and sometimes the market value.

4.2   Ad Valorem Duties

4.2   The following are the ad valorem duties described in detail under the headings listed.

Heading	*Approximate rate of duty*
BEARER INSTRUMENTS (13)—Inland	1.5%
—Overseas	1.5%
—Deposit certificate for overseas stock etc.	0.2%
CLEARANCE SERVICES (22)	1–1.5%
CONVEYANCE OR TRANSFER (28) on sale—Generally	1.0%
—Stock and marketable securities	0.5%
DEPOSITARY RECEIPTS (34)	1–1.5%
EXCHANGE OR PARTITION (37)—Freehold land only	1.0%
LEASES (53)—Rent	1–24.0%
—Premium	1.0%

These rates are approximate because the rates are actually expressed as monetary amounts rather than percentages e.g. '£1 for every £100 or part of £100 of the consideration' instead of 1%, there are sliding scales for some duties and in the case of a CONVEYANCE OR TRANSFER (28) on sale there is an exemption for sales of £60,000 or less when the instrument bears a CERTIFICATE OF VALUE (19). The £60,000 exemption is not available for sales of stock and marketable securities.

5   Agreement for Lease

5.1   An agreement for a lease for any term is charged to duty as if it were an actual lease made for the same term and consideration mentioned in the agreement. [*SA, s 75(1)*]. A lease subsequently granted which conforms with the agreement or is related to substantially the same property and term as the agreement is chargeable to duty; however credit is given for the duty paid on the agreement. [*SA, s 75(2)*].

5.2   Duty paid on an agreement for a lease is not repayable if the lease is not subsequently granted or if the duty on the agreement turns out to be more than the duty on the subsequent lease due to the operation of the

CONTINGENCY PRINCIPLE (26). Although duty paid on an agreement for lease is available as a credit against duty on the lease the credit does not operate the other way round. That is to say duty on the lease cannot be transferred to the agreement.

5.3 Leases executed on or after 6 May 1994 must either contain a certificate (in the form suggested by the Stamp Office—see below) to the effect that there was no prior agreement or be stamped with a stamp denoting either that the agreement is not chargeable with duty or the duty paid on the agreement. [*FA 1994, s 240*].

Agreements for lease executed on or after 6 May 1994 can be submitted with the lease without a penalty for late stamping, provided that they are submitted within 30 days of the date of execution of the lease. Where both lease and agreement are submitted more than 30 days after execution of the lease, the penalty provisions will be applied to both documents. However, the penalty on the agreement will be calculated from the date of execution of the lease, not the date the agreement was executed.

The certificate included in a lease to which there was no agreement should be along the following lines:

'I/We certify that there is no agreement for lease (or tack) to which this lease or tack gives effect.'

In the absence of a certificate the Stamp Office will decline to stamp the lease unless it is accompanied by the agreement for lease.

5.4 Where a freehold or leasehold interest in land is conveyed subject to an agreement for a lease for a term exceeding 35 years, the conveyance must bear a DENOTING STAMP (33) denoting the duty paid on the agreement for lease. This does not apply when the agreement for lease is directly enforceable against another interest in the land. [*FA 1984, s 111(2)(3)*].

5.5 An agreement for a lease for a term of seven years or more must be produced to the Commissioners and stamped with a PRODUCED STAMP (66). [*FA 1931, s 28*].

5.6 Until *FA 1984, s 111* an agreement for a lease for a term exceeding 35 years was exempt from duty and this exemption was exploited in an attempt to mitigate duty on sales of houses. *FA 1984, s 111*, by bringing agreements for leases for more than 35 years within the charge to duty, put an end to the avoidance schemes as did the decision in *Ingram v CIR Ch D, [1985] STC 835*. See 8 ANTI-AVOIDANCE.

5.7 Under *FA 1995, s 151* an agreement for lease between ASSOCIATED COMPANIES (12) is exempt from duty subject to the requirements of that section. See 12.8 ASSOCIATED COMPANIES.

6 Agreement for Sale

6.1 Certain agreements or contracts for sale are charged to ad valorem duty as if they were a CONVEYANCE OR TRANSFER (28) on sale.

6.2 A contract or agreement for sale operates to transfer beneficial ownership but is not a CONVEYANCE OR TRANSFER (28) because it looks forward to subsequent specific performance (*CIR v Angus & Co CA, (1889) 23 QBD 579*).

6.3 But a contract or agreement for sale of

(*a*) any equitable interest in any property, or

(*b*) any estate or interest in any property except

  (i) land

  (ii) property locally situate outside the UK

  (iii) goods, wares or merchandise

  (iv) stock or marketable securities

  (v) ships, vessels or part interest therein

is charged with ad valorem duty, as if it were an actual conveyance on sale. [*SA, s 59(1)*]. See *Farmer & Co v CIR QB, [1898] 2 QB 141*. For calculations of the duty see 28 CONVEYANCE OR TRANSFER.

6.4 Because of these widely drawn exclusions relatively few types of sale agreement attract duty under *Sec 59* but the following contracts and agreements for sale have been held to be liable.

(*a*) An agreement for the sale of GOODWILL (48) (e.g. *West London Syndicate v CIR CA, [1898] 2 QB 507*); but if the goodwill relates to a business carried on entirely outside the UK the agreement is exempt under 6.3(*b*)(ii) above (*Muller & Co's Margarine Ltd v CIR HL, [1901] AC 217*; cf. *Benjamin Brooke & Co v CIR QB, [1896] 2 QB 356*).

(*b*) An agreement to exchange shares in one company in return for an issue of shares in another company where the shares in the first company were to be held on trust for the second company was either a conveyance on sale of an equitable interest or an agreement to sell it (*Chesterfield Brewery Co v CIR QB, [1899] 2 QB 7*).

(*c*) An acknowledgement of receipt given by a reversioner for money in respect of his reversionary interest was an agreement for sale of the reversionary interest. (*Fleetwood-Hesketh v CIR CA, [1936] 1 KB 351*).

(*d*) An agreement for the sale of tenant's fixtures (see *Lee v Gaskell QB, [1876] 1 QBD 700*).

10

6.5   An agreement creating an option to purchase is not liable under *Sec 59*, but may be liable to duty as a CONVEYANCE OR TRANSFER (28) on sale. But an agreement for the sale of a subsisting option may attract duty under *Sec 59*. (*George Wimpey & Co Ltd v CIR CA, [1975] 2 All ER 45*). See 59 OPTIONS AND EQUITY WARRANTS.

6.6   'Property locally situate outside the UK' includes the benefit of a contract enforceable against a non-resident. An agreement for the sale of debts owing by a non-resident debtor is therefore exempt. (*English, Scottish and Australian Bank Ltd v CIR HL, [1932] AC 238*).

6.7   The following points arise in connection with **agreements for the sale of businesses**.

   (*a*)   Where a number of assets (some of which do not attract duty under *Sec 59*) are acquired for one consideration, a bona fide apportionment must be made of the consideration. Stamps form no 22 is used to apportion the consideration.

   (*b*)   Although cash at bank is a debt from a banker and liable to ad valorem duty if agreed to be sold, duty is not in practice claimed on current accounts.

   (*c*)   An agreement to sell debts as at a prior date attracts ad valorem duty on the amount of the debts at that date and not the amount outstanding at the date of the agreement (*Measures Brothers v CIR QB, (1900) 82 LT 689*). Duty may be avoided by arranging for the book debts to be collected on behalf of the vendor and used to discharge his liabilities, providing that any surplus belongs to the vendor and there is no undertaking by the purchaser to make good any deficiency.

   (*d*)   A written contract of sale to a limited company in consideration of the issue of shares is required to be filed, duly stamped, with the Registrar of Companies within one month. [*Companies Act 1985, s 88(2)*]. Where the transaction is concluded by an oral contract, written particulars, stamped as an agreement, must be filed instead. [*ibid, s 88(3)*]. This can be avoided by contracting orally to sell the business for cash and using that consideration to pay for the shares by way of set-off (*Re Harmony and Montague Tin & Copper Mining Co, Spargo's Case CA, (1873) 8 Ch App 407*).

6.8   Where an agreement for sale falls within one of the exclusions (6.3(*b*)(i)–(v) above), it may be possible to complete the transaction without attracting ad valorem duty as a CONVEYANCE OR TRANSFER (28) on sale. See 60 ORAL TRANSACTIONS.

6.9   A subsequent conveyance or transfer made to a purchaser or another person on his behalf does not attract further duty if the agreement is duly stamped ad valorem. The Commissioners will stamp the conveyance with a stamp denoting that ad valorem duty has been paid or transfer the ad valorem duty from the agreement to the conveyance or transfer. [*SA, s 59(3)*]. See 33 DENOTING STAMP.

6.10   An agreement need not be stamped under *Sec 59* if a conveyance or transfer in conformity with the agreement is presented for stamping within six months of the execution of the agreement (or a longer time at the discretion of the Commissioners) and the agreement would not be chargeable with duty apart from *Sec 59*. The conveyance or transfer then bears the ad valorem duty and the agreement is deemed duly stamped. [*SA, s 59(5); FA 1970, 7 Sch 1(3)(b); FA 1985, 27 Sch Pt IX(2)*].

6.11   Where ad valorem duty is paid on an agreement which is later rescinded or not carried into effect so as to operate or be followed by a conveyance or transfer, the duty will be refunded. [*SA, s 59(6)*].

6.12   **AGREEMENT FOR SUB-SALE**

Where the purchaser has paid ad valorem duty on an agreement for sale and before obtaining a conveyance or transfer of the property enters into an agreement for sale of the same, duty on the second agreement is payable as follows:

(*a*)   where the sub-sale consideration is greater than the original consideration—ad valorem duty on the difference;

(*b*)   in any other case—no duty.

[*SA, s 59(2); FA 1970, 7 Sch 1(3)(b); FA 1985, 27 Sch Pt IX(2)*].

A subsequent conveyance or transfer to the sub-purchaser or another person on his behalf attracts no further duty as in 6.9 above.

6.13   If exemption from duty on an agreement under one of the exclusions (6.3(*b*)(i)–(v) above) is claimed, ADJUDICATION (2) may be necessary in order to ensure that the correct amount of duty has been paid.

6.14   Certain agreements for the lease of land are charged with lease duty as actual leases. [*SA, s 75*]. See 5 AGREEMENT FOR LEASE.

7   Annuities

7.1   Annuities are not charged to duty under a separate head and the charges are found as follows.

(*a*)   The creation and sale of annuities other than purchased life and superannuation annuities are charged under the head CONVEYANCE OR TRANSFER (28) on sale.

(b) The conveyance or transfer in consideration of annuities. For the valuation of consideration consisting of an annuity see 25.4 CONSIDERATION.

7.2   PURCHASED LIFE AND SUPERANNUATION ANNUITIES

These are now exempt from duty. [*FA 1989, s 173(2)*].

7.3   OTHER ANNUITIES

The creation and sale of an annuity effected by actual grant or conveyance is charged to ad valorem duty as a CONVEYANCE OR TRANSFER (28) on sale. If the annuity is merely secured by a bond or similar instrument, that document is deemed to be a conveyance on sale. See generally 28 CONVEYANCE OR TRANSFER. [*SA, s 60*].

It has been held that *Sec 60* does not apply to a term annuity (*Commercial Union Assurance Co v CIR KB 1937, [1938] 2 KB 551*). It does apply to the purchase of a perpetual annuity described as a borrowing (*Mersey Docks and Harbour Board v CIR CA, [1897] 2 QB 316*) and to a deed of covenant to make annual payments out of income in exchange for the issue of shares (*Faber v CIR KB, (1936) 155 LT 228*).

7.4   SALE IN CONSIDERATION OF AN ANNUITY

There are special rules for valuing sale consideration consisting of periodic sums, including annuities. See 25.4 CONSIDERATION.

The sale of an annuity and a sale in consideration of an annuity must be distinguished. An instrument securing an annuity in consideration for the transfer of property is treated as a sale in consideration of an annuity (*Blandy v Herbert KB, (1829) 9 B & C 396; Mestayer v Biggs Ex, (1834) 1 CM & R 110*; cf. *Faber v CIR*, above).

---

8   Anti-Avoidance

8.1   In *Ingram v CIR Ch D, [1985] STC 835* it was held that the new approach to tax avoidance as developed by the House of Lords in *W T Ramsay Ltd v CIR [1982] AC 300* and *Furniss v Dawson, [1984] STC 153*, applied to stamp duty.

8.2   In *Ingram* the taxpayer agreed to buy a freehold house for £145,500. In an attempt to reduce the stamp duty payable on this purchase the taxpayer and the vendor entered into an artificial scheme which relied on the fact that an

8.3   Anti-avoidance

AGREEMENT FOR LEASE (5) for more than 35 years did not attract stamp duty [*SA, s 59(1), 75(1)*]. This scheme was subsequently stopped by *FA 1984, s 111*. Under the scheme

(*a*) the vendor and the taxpayer entered into an agreement for the lease of the house for 999 years for a premium of £145,000 and an annual rent of £25;

(*b*) a company owned by the taxpayer's solicitors then agreed to buy the freehold of the house from the vendor for £500;

(*c*) the company then agreed to sub-sell the freehold to the taxpayer for £600;

(*d*) the vendor then conveyed, and the company confirmed, the freehold to the taxpayer.

The taxpayer presented the conveyance for ADJUDICATION (2) contending that stamp duty was chargeable only on the sub-sale consideration of £600, the agreement for the lease being exempt from duty. [*SA, ss 3, 58(4), 59(1), 75(1)*]. The duty was assessed instead on £145,600 i.e. £1,456. The taxpayer appealed to the Chancery Division which held that although stamp duty was a tax on instruments rather than transactions, it was the substance of the transaction that determined the charge to duty. The new approach to tax avoidance applied and the agreement for the lease would be ignored and the two agreements for the sale of the freehold would be treated as an agreement for the sale of the unencumbered freehold to the taxpayer for £145,600, giving rise to stamp duty of £1,456.

8.3   Despite the decision in *Ingram* the application of the new approach to stamp duty will not always be easy. For example, whatever the substance of the transaction there must be in existence an instrument for the Commissioners to stamp and that instrument must fall under one of the heads of charge in the legislation. Moreover, the three cases *Craven v White, CIR v Bowater Property Development Ltd* and *Bayliss v Gregory HL, [1988] STC 476* confirm that the new approach cannot apply where it is not known at the outset that all the transactions in a series of transactions will actually occur.

Since then there has been a further narrowing of the new approach with the courts emphasising that it is really concerned with ascertaining the true legal nature of the transaction and then correctly applying the relevant statutory taxing provisions to it instead of rewriting the transaction (*Ensign Tankers (Leasing) Ltd v Stokes, [1991] STC 136*). Indeed, even this narrower approach may prove embarrassing for the Stamp Office following the issue of the Press Release of 18 April 1994 which in relation to the new ad valorem charge on exchanges of interests in land contained in *FA 1994, s 241* (see 25.8 CONSIDERATION), contains official guidance on how to draft the documentation so as to avoid the multiple charges to duty which were originally intended to be levied.

14

8.4 **STATUTORY ANTI-AVOIDANCE**

(*a*) Every instrument must be written in such a way that the stamp may appear on the face of the instrument and cannot be used for any other instrument written on the same piece of material. [*SA, s 3(1)*].

(*b*) More than one instrument may be written on the same piece of material but each instrument must be separately stamped with its own duty. [*SA, s 3(2)*; but see *FA 1988, s 143(7)*]. A memorandum endorsed on an assurance policy to rectify a mistake in the instrument was a separate instrument liable to duty (*Prudential Assurance Co Ltd v CIR KB, [1935] 1 KB 101*).

(*c*) All the facts and circumstances affecting the liability to duty must be set out in the instrument. [*SA, s 5*]. In practice any facts and circumstances not set out in the instrument can be disclosed in a covering letter to the Commissioners.

(*d*) Three statutory charges referred to by the Chancellor as anti-avoidance measures were introduced by *FA 1994* for documents executed on or after 8 December 1993 (see 25.7 and 25.8 CONSIDERATION; 37 EXCHANGE OR PARTITION; 26 CONTINGENCY PRINCIPLE; and 53.7(b) LEASES). [*FA 1994, ss 241, 242 and 243*].

---

9 Appeals

9.1 Any person who is dissatisfied with an assessment by the Commissioners may, within 21 days of the date of the assessment and after paying the duty assessed, appeal to the High Court. [*SA, s 13(1)*]. The Stamp Office in practice nearly always issues a provisional assessment first and will only issue a (final) assessment once it is clear that agreement on the amount of duty payable is not possible. It is the issue of the (final) assessment which gives rise to the right of appeal. An assessment is made as part of the ADJUDI-CATION (2) procedure.

The Commissioners must then state and sign a case and deliver it to the appellant. In practice the case is normally agreed in draft beforehand. The appellant may then set the appeal down for a hearing within seven days. [*SA, s 13(2)*]. The High Court then decides the question and assesses the duty. [*SA, s 13(3)*]. The case is heard in the Chancery Division. Appeals from the High Court lie to the Court of Appeal and then, with leave, to the House of Lords.

9.2 Appeals

The court may order the repayment of any excess duty paid together with any fine or penalty paid. [*SA, s 13(4)*]. The court may also order interest to be paid to the appellant on any sum repaid. [*FA 1965, s 91*]. Interest has been awarded to run from the date of overpayment (*Crane Fruehauf Ltd v CIR Ch D, [1974] 1 All ER 811*).

9.2 There is no provision under which the appellant can be required to pay the excess if the court assesses an amount of duty higher than that assessed by the Commissioners.

9.3 Appeals in relation to STAMP DUTY RESERVE TAX (73) are referred to the Special Commissioners. [*Stamp Duty Reserve Tax Regulations 1986 (SI 1986 No 1711) Regs 8, 9*].

10 Appointments

10.1 The head of charge 'Appointment of a new trustee, and appointment in execution of a power of any property' in *SA, 1 Sch* was abolished by *FA 1985, s 85(1), 24 Sch (b)*.

10.2 An instrument of appointment of a new trustee will, however, attract a maximum duty of 50p if it contains an express declaration vesting the trust property in the new trustee. [*SA, s 62*]. See *Hadgett v CIR Ex D, (1877) 3 Ex D 46*. The 50p duty can, however, be avoided by including the appropriate certificate in the instrument (see 39 EXEMPT INSTRUMENTS). If the instrument of appointment does not expressly vest the trust property in the trustee but relies instead on an implied vesting under the *Trustee Act 1925, s 40*, it will in practice not attract the 50p duty.

10.3 An appointment under a general power of appointment may be liable to ad valorem duty as a conveyance on sale (see 28 CONVEYANCE OR TRANSFER).

11   Assents

11.1   There is no specific head of charge for assents. However, an assent to vest property agreed to be sold by the deceased is liable to ad valorem duty as a conveyance on sale (see 28 CONVEYANCE OR TRANSFER) (*GHR Co v CIR KB, [1943] KB 303*).

11.2   Formerly, ad valorem duty was charged on assents where a pecuniary legacy was satisfied by the transfer of property with the consent of the legatee (see *Dawson v CIR KB(I), [1905] 2 IR 69*; *Jopling v CIR KB, [1940] 2 KB 282*). The transfer was treated as a conveyance on sale because the legatee was entitled to money from the estate. Ad valorem duty could also arise on the appropriation of property by the personal representatives in satisfaction of the surviving spouse's interest in an intestate's estate. Where ad valorem duty was not charged an assent could attract a fixed 50p duty (see 11.4 below).

11.3   An assent which vests property appropriated in satisfaction of a general legacy of money or in satisfaction of any interest of a surviving spouse in an intestate's estate is no longer subject to ad valorem duty as a conveyance on sale. [*Finance Act 1985, s 84(4)–(7)*]. It was, however, necessary to pay a fixed duty of 50p and have the assent adjudicated. This can now be avoided if the appropriate certificate is included in the instrument (see 11.4 below and 39 EXEMPT INSTRUMENTS).

11.4   An assent which gives effect to any of the following transactions and which includes the appropriate certificate is exempt from the fixed duty of 50p and does not have to be adjudicated:

(*a*)   the conveyance or transfer of property the subject of a specific devise or legacy to the beneficiary named in the will (or his nominee);

(*b*)   the conveyance or transfer of property which forms part of an intestate's estate to the person entitled on intestacy (or his nominee);

(*c*)   the appropriation of property within *Finance Act 1985, s 84(4)* or *(5)* or *(7)* (see 11.3 above);

(*d*)   the conveyance or transfer of property which forms part of the residuary estate of a testator to a beneficiary (or his nominee) entitled solely by virtue of his entitlement under the will.

[*Stamp Duty (Exempt Instruments) Regulations 1987 (SI 1987 No 516)*].

See 39 EXEMPT INSTRUMENTS.

12 Associated Companies

Note. This exemption was altered significantly by *FA 1995, s 149* for instruments executed on or after 1 May 1995. For the previous position refer to the third edition of this book.

12.1 EXEMPTION

Stamp duty is not charged under the head CONVEYANCE OR TRANSFER (28) on sale on an instrument provided that:

(*a*) the effect of the instrument is to convey or transfer a beneficial interest in property from one body corporate to another, and

(*b*) the bodies in question are associated at the time the instrument is executed.

To be duly stamped, it is necessary for the instrument of transfer to be stamped either with a stamp denoting that no duty is chargeable or with the duty which is otherwise chargeable under the head CONVEYANCE OR TRANSFER (28) on sale. [*FA 1930, s 42, amended by FA 1995, s 149*]. The exemption has been extended to LEASES (53), AGREEMENT FOR LEASE (5) and an 'agreement with respect to a letting'. [*FA 1995, s 151*]. (See 12.8 below).

12.2 Bodies corporate, wherever incorporated or resident, are associated at a particular time if at that time one is the parent of the other or another body corporate is the parent of each. One body corporate is regarded for this purpose as the parent of another at a particular time if at that time the first body is the beneficial owner of not less than 75% of the ordinary share capital of the second body. 'Ordinary share capital' means all the issued share capital of a body corporate except shares having the right to a dividend at a fixed rate but no other right to share in profits.

In determining whether 75% of the ordinary share capital is held, indirect holdings are counted. Fractional elements through a chain of companies are determined by multiplying the fractions in the chain. [*FA 1938, 4 Sch*].

12.3 **In relation to beneficial ownership** it has been held that

(*a*) an unconditional contract to sell shares in a company will deprive the transferor of beneficial ownership on execution, notwithstanding that conditions remain to be fulfilled prior to completion (*CIR v Ufitec Group Ltd QB, [1977] 3 All ER 924; Parway Estates Ltd v CIR CA, (1958) 45 TC 135*);

(*b*) a conditional contract will pass beneficial ownership where the purchaser can waive the conditions (see at first instance *Wood Preservation Ltd v Prior Ch D, [1968] 2 All ER 849*) or where the vendor is otherwise unable to sell (*Brooklands Selangor Holdings Ltd v CIR Ch D, [1970] 2 All ER 76*);

(c) a company loses beneficial ownership of its assets when it is placed in liquidation (e.g. *Olive Mill Spinners Ltd Ch D, [1963] 2 All ER 130; Ayerst v C & K (Construction) Ltd HL, [1975] 3 WLR 16*);

(d) arrangements to which a company is or is not a party may deprive the company of beneficial ownership (*Holmleigh (Holdings) Ltd v CIR*, above);

(e) the overall effect of a scheme is considered in determining whether and when beneficial ownership passes (e.g. *Leigh Spinners Ltd v CIR Ch D, (1956) 35 ATC 58*).

12.4   For the exemption to apply the effect of the instrument must be to convey or transfer a beneficial interest in the property from the transferor to the transferee. It often happens that a sale agreement is entered into prior to the formal conveyance and the beneficial interest passes not by the conveyance but by implication on the sale agreement being entered into. In such cases it has been held that the conveyance or transfer attracts the relief because it is to be stamped according to the value of the beneficial interest which passed from the seller to the buyer under the sale agreement. See *Escoigne Properties Ltd v CIR HL, [1958] AC 549 at 563, 564.*

12.5   LOSS OF EXEMPTION

The exemption is not available unless it is shown to the Commissioners' satisfaction that the instrument was not executed as part of any of the following types of arrangement.

(a) The consideration or part of the consideration for the transfer was to be provided or received, directly or indirectly, by a person other than a company itself associated with either the transferor or transferee. In particular, this extends to arrangements whereby the transferor or transferee company or another associated company was enabled to provide any of the consideration or was to part with any of it by carrying out a transaction involving a payment or other disposition by a person other than an associated company. Bank borrowing on normal commercial terms with no obligation in the loan agreement to apply the loan in a particular way or to repay the loan out of sales proceeds of the property purchased, is not regarded as an 'arrangement'. In the Standing Committee debates on the 1995 Finance Bill the Minister of State at the Treasury stated that the exemption would not be available if a loan was taken out specifically for the purpose of financing the transfer and was secured on the assets transferred. However, a general purpose loan which the borrower could apply in any way it chose would not jeopardise the exemption (Hansard Committee D, Twentieth Sitting, 7 March 1995, cols 620–621).

For examples of arrangements which would now be caught by this provision see *Shop and Store Developments Ltd v CIR HL, [1967] 1 AC 472; Curzon Offices Ltd v CIR CA, [1944] 1 All ER 606.*

12.6 Associated Companies

(b) The beneficial interest was previously conveyed or transferred, directly or indirectly, by a person other than an associated company. 'Conveyed or transferred' has been widely construed to include the passing of the beneficial interest in property to a purchaser where the property was sub-sold and the conveyance taken direct to the sub-purchaser (*Escoigne Properties Ltd v CIR HL, [1958] AC 549*), and the transfer of the beneficial interest in property by a lease (*Littlewoods Mail Order Stores Ltd v CIR HL, [1963] AC 135*).

(c) The transferor and transferee were to cease to be associated by reason of the transferor or third body corporate ceasing to be the transferee's parent (within the meaning of 12.2 above). For an example of an arrangement now caught by this provision, see *Times Newspapers Ltd v CIR Ch D, [1971] 3 All ER 98*. This provision can apply where there are arrangements for the transferee to leave the 75% group but it will not normally apply where the transferor is leaving the 75% group. The fact that the property is being sold within the group in preparation for a possible sale of the shares in the transferee company outside the group ought not to prevent the exemption being available.

[*FA 1967, s 27*].

12.6 PROCEDURE

ADJUDICATION (2) is required for any instrument for which exemption is claimed. It is also necessary to submit a statutory declaration setting out the facts justifying the claim for relief. The Commissioners publish a helpful information sheet on how to apply for the relief and this sheet is reproduced in 79 PRACTICAL MATERIALS together with a specimen statutory declaration.

12.7 STAMP DUTY RESERVE TAX

There is no equivalent exemption from STAMP DUTY RESERVE TAX (73) for transfers of shares between associated companies. However, if the stock transfer form is adjudicated and exemption from stamp duty is given under *FA 1930, s 42* no stamp duty reserve tax will be payable. If stamp duty reserve tax has been paid within the previous six years it can be reclaimed. Where a stock transfer form is not executed and subsequently adjudicated and the intra-group share transfer effected merely on the basis of a board minute or a declaration of trust, stamp duty reserve tax is, strictly speaking, payable. It is therefore necessary to have each intra-group share transfer completed by a transfer which is adjudicated if a charge to stamp duty reserve tax is to be avoided. See 73 STAMP DUTY RESERVE TAX.

12.8 LEASES ETC.

The associated company exemption has been extended to LEASES (53), AGREEMENT FOR LEASE (5) and 'agreements with respect to a letting' in relation to instruments executed on or after 1 May 1995. [*FA 1995, s 151*].

Stamp duty is not charged under the head 'Lease or Tack' provided that:

(*a*) the lessor is a body corporate and the lessee is another body corporate,

(*b*) those bodies are associated at the time the instrument is executed,

(*c*) in the case of an agreement, the agreement is for the lease or tack or letting to be granted to the lessee or to a body corporate associated with the lessee at the time the instrument is executed, and

(*d*) the instrument is not executed in pursuance of or in connection with an arrangement of the sort described in 12.5 (*a*) and (*c*) above (for 'transferor' and 'transferee' read 'lessor' and 'lessee'). 'Lessor' means the person granting the lease or tack or agreeing to grant the lease, tack or letting. 'Lessee' means the person granted the lease or tack or agreeing for the lease, tack or letting to be granted to him or another. [*FA 1995, s 151(6)*].

To be duly stamped it is necessary for the instrument of transfer to be stamped either with a stamp denoting that no duty is chargeable or with the duty which is otherwise chargeable under the head 'Lease or Tack'. [*FA 1995, s 151(5)*].

12.9 Whether bodies corporate are associated is decided according to the same criteria as set out in 12.2 above.

12.10 It will be noted that in contrast with the exemption under *FA 1930, s 42* (see 12.1 above) there is no requirement that the lease should be beneficially owned by the lessor or any other associated company although it is thought that the Stamp Office would resist granting the exemption where this was exploited by the use of a nominee lessor acting for a non-associated person.

---

13   Bearer Instruments

Note. This head of duty was to be abolished with effect from a date to be appointed by statutory instrument. [*FA 1990, ss 107, 111*]. But see 1.1 INTRODUCTION.

13.1 The head 'Bearer Instrument' was inserted into *SA, 1 Sch* by *FA 1963, s 59*. As bearer instruments can be transferred by delivery, the charge to stamp duty is on issue or in certain cases on first transfer in the UK. As amended by *FA 1967, s 30* and *FA 1987, s 51*, the charge applies only to bearer instruments expressed in sterling. Bearer instrument duty is not chargeable on bearer instruments expressed in a foreign currency or in units of account relating to more than one currency.

13.2   Bearer Instruments

13.2   INSTRUMENTS CHARGED AND RATES OF DUTY

(*a*) **Inland bearer instrument** (other than a deposit certificate for overseas stock)—three times the *transfer duty* i.e. 1.5%.

(*b*) **Overseas bearer instrument** (other than a deposit certificate for overseas stock or bearer instrument by usage)—three times the *transfer duty* i.e. 1.5%.

(*c*) **Inland or overseas deposit certificate for overseas stock or bearer instrument by usage**—10p for every £50 or part £50 of market value (see 13.6 below).

(*d*) **Inland or overseas bearer instrument given in substitution for a like instrument duly stamped ad valorem**—fixed duty of 10p.

Transfer duty is the amount of duty which would be chargeable on a conveyance or transfer on sale of the bearer instrument at its market value by a written instrument of transfer. [*FA 1963, s 59(3)*]. (See 13.6 below).

13.3   DEFINITIONS

(*a*) An *inland bearer instrument* is an instrument issued by or on behalf of a company or body of persons formed or established in the UK, which is

  (i) a marketable security transferable by delivery,

  (ii) a share warrant or stock certificate to bearer or similar instrument,

  (iii) a deposit certificate to bearer, or

  (iv) any other bearer instrument by which stock can be transferred.

(*b*) An *overseas bearer instrument* is an instrument as in (*a*) issued by a company or body of persons not formed or established in the UK, or a bearer instrument by usage issued by such persons.

(*c*) A *deposit certificate* is an instrument acknowledging the deposit of stock and entitling the bearer to rights in that or equivalent stock.

(*d*) A *deposit certificate for overseas stock* is a deposit certificate as in (*c*) in respect of stock of one company or body of persons formed or established outside the UK.

(*e*) A *bearer instrument by usage* is an instrument not otherwise treated as a bearer instrument, delivery of which is treated by usage as sufficient for sale on the market, whether or not delivery constitutes a legal transfer.

(*f*) *Stock* is widely defined as including securities, rights and interests in stock (including fractions) and rights to an allotment of or subscription to stock.

[*FA 1963, s 59(2)(4)*].

22

13.4 OCCASIONS OF CHARGE

(*a*) **On issue**

The following bearer instruments attract duty on *issue*

(i) any instrument *issued* in the UK,

(ii) any instrument *issued* by or on behalf of a company or body of persons formed or established in GB, other than a *foreign loan security* i.e. a security *issued* outside the UK in respect of a loan expressed in a currency other than sterling and which is neither offered for subscription in the UK nor offered with a view to an offer for sale in the UK.

Issue in this context occurs when and where the instrument gets into the hands of a person who can avail himself of it (*Baring Bros v CIR QB, [1898] 1 QB 78*).

(*b*) **On transfer**

Instruments not chargeable under (*a*) above are chargeable on first (but not subsequent) transfer (including negotiation) in GB, but only if the transfer would be chargeable with conveyance on sale duty if the transfer were by an instrument other than a bearer instrument. [*FA 1963, s 60*].

13.5 STAMPING PROCEDURE

Different procedures apply to instruments chargeable on issue and on transfer. [*FA 1963, s 60*].

(*a*) **Instruments chargeable on issue** must be delivered to the Commissioners before issue for the instrument to be stamped with a DENOTING STAMP (33) denoting that it has been produced. The instrument is not duly stamped unless it bears this denoting stamp, but the duty is not payable until six weeks after issue, when a statement must be delivered to the Commissioners.

(*b*) **Instruments chargeable on transfer** must be presented to the Commissioners for stamping before transfer and they will then be deemed to be duly stamped.

(*c*) **Substituted bearer instruments** should be presented to the Commissioners either on issue or on transfer as appropriate together with the original instruments. In order to be duly stamped the substituted instrument must be stamped with a DENOTING STAMP (33) as in (*a*) above if it is chargeable on issue or with a stamp denoting 'original security duly stamped' if it is chargeable on transfer.

There are fines for failure to comply with these requirements. See 64 PENALTIES AND OFFENCES.

13.6   Bearer Instruments

13.6 VALUATION

Ad valorem duty on a bearer instrument is calculated on its market value. [*FA 1963, s 61*]. Market value is ascertained as follows.

(*a*) **Instrument chargeable on issue**

    (i) Where the underlying stock was offered for public subscription (whether in registered or bearer form) within twelve months before the issue of the bearer instrument—the amount subscribed.

    (ii) If the underlying stock was not so offered for public subscription but is dealt in on The International Stock Exchange within one month of the issue of the instrument—its value on the first day of dealing.

    (iii) In any other case—its value immediately after issue.

(*b*) **Instrument chargeable on transfer**

    (i) Transfer pursuant to a contract of sale—its value on the date of the contract. The contract price under an arm's length contract will normally be used.

    (ii) In any other case—the value on the day preceding presentation to the Commissioners for stamping; if it is not so presented—the value on the date of transfer.

13.7 EXEMPTIONS

(*a*) **Non-sterling currency stock.** Duty is not charged on bearer instruments relating to stock expressed in a foreign currency or in units of account relating to more than one currency. If the instrument relates to a loan and repayment could, at the option of the holder only, be made in a foreign currency, it qualifies for exemption. Instruments relating to the capital stock of companies or bodies which is not expressed in any currency (e.g. shares of no par value) are treated as if they were expressed in the currency of the territory under the law of which the company or body is formed or established. Units in a unit trust scheme or a share in a foreign mutual fund are treated as if they were capital stock of a company or body formed or established in the country whose law governs the scheme or fund. [*FA 1967, s 30; FA 1987, s 51*]. This exemption and the equivalent exemption from STAMP DUTY RESERVE TAX (73) in *FA 1986, s 90(3)(b)* have been used successfully to avoid ad valorem duty on sales of the shares of UK companies under the scheme described in 72.4(*a*) SHARES AND SECURITIES.

(*b*) **Renounceable letters of allotment**, letters of rights and similar instruments, e.g. renounceable letters of acceptance, where the rights are renounceable not later than six months after issue, are exempt. [*FA 1963, s 59; SA, 1 Sch*]. Such a document is also exempt from duty as a CONVEYANCE OR TRANSFER (28) on sale, except in relation to arrangements where rights to company shares under an instrument are renounced in favour of someone, who together with persons connected with him, has or will have control of the company as a result of the arrangements. [*FA 1963, s 65(1); FA 1985, s 81*]. The exception to the conveyance on sale exemption was directed at a version of the 'pref-trick' which practitioners had developed to counter the decision in *Furniss v Dawson, [1984] STC 153.* (See 8 ANTI-AVOIDANCE.) It is considered, however, that a letter of allotment may not attract duty as a CONVEYANCE OR TRANSFER (28) on sale because it is not a transfer. It is the delivery of the letter that effects a transfer and not the letter itself.

Dealings in renounceable letters of allotment etc. do, however, attract STAMP DUTY RESERVE TAX (73), except in relation to overseas bearer instruments. [*FA 1986, ss 87, 90(3)*]. See also 54 LETTERS OF ALLOTMENT AND ACCEPTANCE.

(*c*) **Government stocks etc.** Bearer instruments relating to Government stocks and other stocks exempt from all stamp duties are themselves exempt. For details of stocks covered by exemptions, see 39 EXEMPT INSTRUMENTS. [*FA 1963, s 59; SA, 1 Sch*].

(*d*) LOAN CAPITAL AND DEBENTURES (55). Duty is not charged on the issue or transfer of all forms of bearer loan capital. [*FA 1986, s 79(2)*].

(*e*) **Variations of overseas bearer instruments** in respect of a loan expressed in sterling do not bear duty provided that the original has been duly stamped. [*FA 1970, 7 Sch 6(4)*].

(*f*) DEPOSITARY RECEIPTS (34) and CLEARANCE SERVICES (22). The transfer, issue or appropriation of an inland bearer instrument (except a renounceable letter of allotment) into a depositary scheme or a clearance service is exempt from STAMP DUTY RESERVE TAX (73). [*FA 1986, ss 95(2), 97(3)*].

(*g*) **Paired shares.** Exemption from duty is available on the issue of units and warrants to acquire units of the type issued by Eurotunnel. [*FA 1988, s 143*].

14   Bills of Exchange

14.1   The head of charge 'Bill of Exchange or Promissory Note' in *SA, 1 Sch* was abolished by *FA 1970, 7 Sch 2*. This head formerly covered bills of exchange, cheques and promissory notes. Such documents are now unlikely to attract any stamp duty.

15   Bills of Sale

15.1   An absolute bill of sale is liable to duty as a CONVEYANCE OR TRANSFER (28) on sale. [*SA, 1 Sch*].

15.2   A bill of sale cannot be registered unless a duly stamped original is produced to the proper officer. [*SA, s 41*].

16   Bonds

16.1   Nearly all the 'Bond' headings in *SA, 1 Sch* no longer exist. [*FA 1971, s 64; FA 1973, 22 Sch; FA 1989, s 173*]. Bonds and covenants in relation to an annuity on the original creation and sale of the annuity are charged under the head CONVEYANCE OR TRANSFER (28) on sale (see 7 ANNUITIES). [*SA, 1 Sch*].

16.2   The head 'Bond, Covenant' formerly charged bonds, covenants and similar instruments and extended to

(*a*)   a principal or primary security for an annuity (other than a superannuation annuity or on original creation by sale or security) or for periodic sums of money (other than interest on principal secured by a duly stamped agreement or rent reserved by a lease), e.g. a seven-year deed of covenant, and

(*b*)   a collateral or substituted security for annuities or periodic sums as in (*a*).

These duties were abolished *except* as regards documents increasing rent [*FA 1971, s 64(1)(a)*] which are charged under the head 'Bond, Covenant' but attract lease duty. [*SA, s 77(5)*]. See 53 LEASES.

16.3   The duty charged on superannuation annuities and purchased life annuities under paragraph (3) of the head 'Bond, Covenant' was abolished by *FA 1989, s 173*.

16.4   The miscellaneous head 'Bond of any kind whatsoever not specifically charged with any duty' has also been abolished. [*FA 1971, s 64(1)(b)*].

16.5   **Exemption from other duties.** The documents formerly charged under the heads described above do not now attract duty under any other head unless an instrument contains several distinct matters (see 52 LEADING AND PRINCIPAL OBJECT), when it will only be exempt to the extent that it falls within the former head of charge. [*FA 1971, s 64(2); FA 1989, s 173(2)*].

16.6 Bonds for securing the payment of money or the transfer or retransfer of stock were formerly charged under the head 'Marketable Security', but that head of charge has been abolished. [*FA 1973, 22 Sch*].

17 Building Societies

17.1 The following instruments are exempt from all stamp duties:

(*a*) any copy of the rules of a building society;

(*b*) any transfer of a share in a building society;

(*c*) any bond or other security given to, or on account of a building society;

(*d*) any instrument appointing an agent of a building society or revoking such an appointment; and

(*e*) any other instrument whatsoever which is required or authorised to be given, issued, signed, made or produced pursuant to the Building Societies Act 1986 or the rules of a building society.

[*Building Societies Act 1986, s 109(1)*].

17.2 **CONVERSION TO A PUBLIC LIMITED COMPANY**

No stamp duty liability can arise on the transfer of the business of a building society to a successor company effected under the *Building Societies Act 1986, s 97(6) or (7)*. [*Building Societies Act 1986, s 109(2); FA 1988, s 145, 12 Sch 8*].

18 Capital Duty

18.1 Capital duty was abolished with effect from 16 March 1988. [*FA 1988, s 141*].

The duty was charged at the rate of 1% on the documents relating to increases in the capital of certain types of company and to various other transactions involving such companies.

19 Certificate of Value

19.1 A certificate of value is required where nil duty is claimed in respect of a transaction otherwise attracting ad valorem duty under the head CONVEYANCE OR TRANSFER (28) on sale. This includes

(*a*) conveyances or transfers on sale;

(*b*) equality money paid on an EXCHANGE OR PARTITION (37);

(*c*) premiums paid under LEASES (53).

[*FA 1963, s 55(1); FA 1958, s 34(4)*].

An instrument containing a certificate of value does not need to be presented for stamping.

19.2 A certificate of value cannot be given for

(i) a lease where the consideration includes rent exceeding £600 p.a.; or

(ii) transfers of stock or marketable securities.

[*FA 1963, s 55(1A)(2)*].

19.3 An instrument is 'certified at' a particular amount if it contains a statement that the transaction effected by the instrument does not form part of a larger transaction or series of transactions in which the total amount or value of the consideration exceeds the certified amount, currently £60,000. [*FA 1958, s 34(4); FA 1993, s 201*]. For documents executed on or after 20 December 1991 and before 20 August 1992 the certified amount was temporarily increased from £30,000 to £250,000. [*Stamp Duty (Temporary Provisions) Act 1992*]. For documents executed on or after 20 August 1992 and before 16 March 1993 the certified amount was £30,000. For the calculation of the amount or value of the consideration see CONSIDERATION (25). Where the value cannot be determined at the time of the certificate, a truncated certificate can be given certifying that the transaction does not form part of a larger transaction or series of transactions and that the correct amount of duty will be applied when the amount or value of the consideration is determined. Although the certificate should appear in the instrument, the Commissioners may permit the addition of a certificate at a later stage if it is signed by the parties who executed the instrument.

19.4 Stock etc. is ignored when deciding if a certificate of value can be given in an instrument chargeable as a CONVEYANCE OR TRANSFER (28) on sale under *SA, s 54*. This is provided that the instrument does not operate as a conveyance or transfer of the stock etc. The same applies to an AGREEMENT FOR SALE (6) chargeable as a conveyance or transfer on sale under *SA, s 59*. [*FA 1958, s 34(4)*]. Transfer of these items can generally be effected by delivery (60 ORAL TRANSACTIONS) attracting no duty and thus they do not affect the duty chargeable on other property included in a sale. But see 19.6 below.

19.5   Whether a transaction forms part of a **larger transaction or series of transactions** depends on the circumstances of each transaction.

The following need not necessarily be so treated:

(*a*)   the purchase of more than one lot at an auction (*A-G v Cohen CA, [1937] 1 KB 478*);

(*b*)   a related transaction which is not a sale (*Kimbers & Co v CIR KB, [1936] 1 KB 132*);

(*c*)   a purchase and sub-sale of property;

(*d*)   a number of acquisitions from different vendors even if each is conditional on completion of the others;

(*e*)   the Stamp Office have stated that the £60,000 threshold can be applied separately to each side of an exchange of properties. However, where there is a multiple exchange of properties e.g. properties A and B are exchanged for property C—the transfers of A and B are regarded as parts of a larger transaction, and the threshold would not apply to either of them if the total consideration for both was more than £60,000. The threshold would be applied separately however to the transfer of C. (Inland Revenue Press Release, 18 April 1994 and see 25.7 CONSIDERATION).

However, where there is more than one transaction negotiated at the same time between two parties, it may be more difficult to show that they do not form part of a larger transaction or series of transactions whether or not they are included in separate contracts (see *A-G v Cohen KB, [1936] 2 KB 246* and *CA, [1937] 1 KB 478*).

19.6   In relation to the use of certificates of value, it was stated in *Saunders v Edwards CA, [1987] 1 WLR 1116 at 1125* that a solicitor involved in an apportionment between the value of the property and that of the chattels, which he knows not to be in accordance with the facts must be guilty of professional misconduct and apart from possible criminal offences, the consequence for the buyers may well be that their contract becomes unenforceable.

19.7   In relation to the use of certificates of value in conveyances or leases of building plots see 25.6 CONSIDERATION.

19.8   A separate certification procedure is available for instruments that would otherwise attract a 50p fixed duty (see 39 EXEMPT INSTRUMENTS).

20 Chargeability

20.1 Stamp duties are charged on INSTRUMENTS (49) [*SA, s 1*] and not on transactions that are carried out orally (see 60 ORAL TRANSACTIONS) or persons as such. STAMP DUTY RESERVE TAX (73) is charged on transactions and not instruments.

20.2 Instruments are chargeable to stamp duty if they are

(*a*) executed in the UK, or

(*b*) executed anywhere, relating to property situate or any matter or thing to be done in the UK.

[*SA, s 14(4)*].

Thus only instruments executed abroad and relating to non-UK matters will be outside the stamp duty charge (but see 39 EXEMPT INSTRUMENTS). It has been held, inter alia, that

(i) a transfer executed in France of French property by an English company to another English company in consideration of shares in that company related to property situate in England (the shares) and was dutiable as a conveyance on sale (see 28 CONVEYANCE OR TRANSFER) (*Maple & Co (Paris) Ltd HL, [1908] AC 22*);

(ii) a covenant executed in Canada whereby, in consideration for a Canadian company issuing shares and debentures, an individual covenanted to pay the company a proportion of his professional income, related to the carrying on of his profession in the UK and was liable to duty (*Faber v CIR KB, (1936) 155 LT 228*).

20.3 Duty is not, however, payable on a chargeable instrument executed outside the UK until it is received in the UK. (See 63.1(*c*) PAYMENT OF DUTY OR TAX.)

21 Charities

21.1 Stamp duty under the 'CONVEYANCE OR TRANSFER (28) on sale', 'Conveyance or transfer of any kind not hereinbefore described' and 'Lease or Tack' headings in *SA, 1 Sch* is not charged on any conveyance, transfer or lease made or agreed to be made to a charity, The Trustees of the National Heritage Memorial Fund, or the Historic Buildings and Monuments Commission for England. [*FA 1982, s 129(1); FA 1983, s 46(3)(c)*]. Similar exemption is not available for conveyances etc. made by a charity.

21.2 For the above exemption to apply it is necessary to have the conveyance etc. adjudicated. [*FA 1982, s 129(2)*]. See 2 ADJUDICATION.

22   Clearance Services

Note. The stamp duty and stamp duty reserve tax charges in relation to clearance services were to be abolished from a date to be appointed by statutory instrument. [*FA 1990, ss 108–111*]. But see 1.1. INTRODUCTION.

22.1 Clearance services exist which allow the shares and securities of UK incorporated companies registered in the name of a nominee to be bought and sold free of stamp duty. A special charge was therefore imposed on the entry of shares or securities into a clearance service to compensate for the non-payment of stamp duty on subsequent purchases and sales of the shares or securities within the service. Generally, the charge is at 1.5%, three times the normal rate of ad valorem duty on CONVEYANCE OR TRANSFER (28) on sale of SHARES AND SECURITIES (72). The special charge can be either stamp duty (see 22.3 below) or STAMP DUTY RESERVE TAX (73) (see 22.4 below) depending on the circumstances.

22.2 The term 'clearance services' is not defined in the relevant legislation. There must be many arrangements relating to the transfer of shares and involving nominee ownership which are potentially within the scope of the special charge. It is thought that the special charge was intended to apply only to the widely used commercial clearance services such as Euroclear and the Commissioners can be expected to limit the application of the special charge accordingly.

22.3 **STAMP DUTY**

Stamp duty at the special rate is charged on an instrument which *transfers* 'relevant securities' of a UK incorporated company to a person

(*a*) whose business consists exclusively of holding shares, stock or marketable securities as nominee or agent for a person whose business is or includes providing a clearance service for the purchase and sale of 'relevant securities'; or

(*b*) who is specified by a statutory instrument and whose business is or includes providing a clearance service; or

(*c*) who is specified by a statutory instrument and whose business does not consist exclusively of holding 'relevant securities' as nominee or agent for a clearer.

31

22.4 Clearance Services

The foreign company is treated as a company incorporated in the UK for 'relevant securities' which consist of units representing paired shares of the type issued by Eurotunnel. [*FA 1986, s 70(1)(6)–(8); FA 1988, s 143(6)*].

'Relevant securities' are shares or stock or marketable securities of any company wherever incorporated. [*FA 1986, s 72(1)*].

Where the instrument of transfer attracts duty under the CONVEYANCE OR TRANSFER (28) on sale head or the 'conveyance or transfer of any kind not hereinbefore described' head, duty is charged at the special rate of £1.50 per £100 or part of £100 of the amount or value of the sale consideration. [*FA 1986, s 70(2)(3)*]. A transfer of 'relevant securities' of a UK incorporated company between corporate nominees resident in the UK attracts only a maximum 50p duty. [*FA 1986, s 70(9)*].

Where the instrument attracts duty under the 'conveyance or transfer of any kind not hereinbefore described' head the special rate is reduced to £1.00 per £100 or part of £100 of the value of the securities where the transferor is a 'qualified dealer' in securities of the kind concerned or his nominee but is not a 'market maker' in those securities and the transfer is in the course of the dealer's business. The instrument must contain a statement to this effect. [*FA 1986, s 70(4)*]. A person is a 'qualified dealer' in securities of a particular kind if he deals in those securities and is a member of a recognised stock exchange within the meaning of *ICTA 1988, s 841* or is designated a 'qualified dealer' by Treasury Order [*FA 1986, s 69(6)*].

A person is a 'market maker' if he holds himself out at all normal times under The International Stock Exchange rules as willing to buy and sell securities of the kind concerned at a price specified by him and is recognised as doing so by the Council of The International Stock Exchange. [*FA 1986, s 69(7)*].

A provider of clearance services relating to 'relevant securities' of UK incorporated companies and a person whose business includes (albeit not exclusively) holding such securities as a nominee or agent for a clearer is required to notify the Commissioners of that fact within one month of providing such services. [*FA 1986, s 71(1)(2)*]. A fine of up to £1,000 can be imposed for failing to do so. [*FA 1986, s 71(4)*]. A UK incorporated company which becomes aware that its shares are held by a clearer or his agent or nominee is also required to notify the Commissioners of that fact within one month of becoming so aware. A fine of up to £100 can be imposed for failing to do so. [*FA 1986, s 71(3)(5)*].

22.4 STAMP DUTY RESERVE TAX

STAMP DUTY RESERVE TAX (73) is charged where 'chargeable securities' are *issued* or *transferred* to a person whose business is or includes providing a clearance service for the purchase and sale of 'chargeable securities' or to his nominee. [*FA 1986, s 96(1)*].

For the definition of 'chargeable securities' see 73 STAMP DUTY RESERVE TAX.

In relation to the *transfer* of 'chargeable securities' any ad valorem stamp duty chargeable on the instrument of transfer (see 22.3 above) cancels the equivalent amount of stamp duty reserve tax chargeable up to the full amount of the reserve tax. [*FA 1986, s 96(5)*].

In the case of the securities being *issued* to a clearer or his nominee stamp duty reserve tax is charged at £1.50 per £100 or part of £100 of the issue price. In the case of securities being *transferred* for money or money's worth the rate is £1.50 per £100 or part of £100 of the amount or value of the consideration. In any other case the rate is £1.50 per £100 or part of £100 of the *value* of the securities. [*FA 1986, s 96(2)*].

In relation to the *transfer* of securities where the instrument of transfer attracts stamp duty under the 'conveyance or transfer of any kind not hereinbefore described' head the special rate of stamp duty reserve tax is reduced to £1.00 per £100 or part of £100 where the transferor is a 'qualified dealer' in securities of the kind concerned or his nominee but is not a 'market maker' in the securities concerned and the transfer is in the course of the dealer's business. The instrument must contain a statement to this effect. [*ibid, s 96(3)*].

A person is a 'qualified dealer' if he is a member of a recognised stock exchange or is designated a qualified dealer by the Treasury. [*FA 1986, ss 93(5), 94(5), 96(11)*].

A person is a 'market maker' if he holds himself out at all normal times under The International Stock Exchange rules as willing to buy and sell securities of the kind concerned at a price specified by him and is recognised as doing so by the Council of The International Stock Exchange. [*FA 1986, ss 93(5), 94(6), 96(11)*].

There are the following exceptions to the tax charge:

(*a*)   a transfer of securities between corporate nominees who are resident in the UK and whose businesses are exclusively that of holding securities as nominees for a clearer;

(*b*)   a transfer of securities to The International Stock Exchange's nominee or to a recognised investment exchange or recognised clearing house or their nominees, on which stamp duty is not chargeable by virtue of *FA 1976, s 127(1)* or *FA 1986, s 84(2) or (3)*;

(*c*)   the transfer or issue of an inland bearer instrument which is not a renounceable letter of allotment with a life of six months or less (see 13 BEARER INSTRUMENTS); and

(*d*)   the *issue* by one company of securities in exchange for shares in another company where the first company has control of the second (or will have control as a result of the exchange).

[*FA 1986, s 97*].

23 Company Reorganisations

23.1 There are four main exemptions and reliefs from stamp duty under the CONVEYANCE OR TRANSFER (28) on sale head of charge for company reorganisations, as follows:

(a) exemption where one company acquires the whole or part of an undertaking of another company under a scheme of reconstruction of that other company (see 23.2 below);

(b) a relief in the form of a reduced rate of ½% on certain other acquisitions by one company of the undertaking of another company (see 23.3 below);

(c) exemption for the placing of a new holding company above an existing company (see 23.4 below);

(d) exemption for internal reorganisations involving the transfer of property within a 75% owned group of companies (see 12 ASSOCIATED COMPANIES).

Also relevant in the context of company reorganisations are the exemptions for transfers in connection with divorce [FA 1985, s 83] and deeds of variation [FA 1985, s 84] where shares in family companies are concerned (see 42 FAMILY ARRANGEMENTS AND DIVORCE).

23.2 **RECONSTRUCTIONS** [FA 1986, s 75]

Exemption from stamp duty under the CONVEYANCE OR TRANSFER (28) on sale head of charge is available where one company ('the acquiring company') acquires the whole or part of an undertaking of another company ('the target company') under a scheme of reconstruction of the target company.

A 'scheme of reconstruction' requires that there is a transfer of the undertaking or part of the undertaking from an existing company to a new company with substantially the same membership as the old company and that the undertaking continues substantially unaltered (Brooklands Selangor Holdings Ltd v CIR Ch D, [1970] 2 All ER 76; Baytrust Holdings Ltd v CIR Ch D, [1971] 3 All ER 76; see also CIR v Kent Process Control Ltd Ch D, [1989] STC 245 and Swithland Investments Ltd v CIR [1990] STC 448).

Under the now repealed FA 1927, s 55 relief was available for schemes of reconstruction and also for schemes of amalgamation of companies. A 'scheme of amalgamation' connotes the merging of two or more businesses with ownership through shareholdings remaining substantially the same (Crane Fruehauf Ltd v CIR CA, [1975] 1 All ER 429; Ufitec Group Ltd v CIR QB, [1977] STC 363). A scheme of amalgamation is therefore quite different from a scheme of reconstruction and the omission of the former from FA 1986, s 75 indicates that relief is limited to schemes of reconstruction.

The relief is subject to the following requirements.

(*a*) The registered office of the acquiring company must be in the UK. Following the decision of the European Court of Justice in *Halliburton Services BV v Staatssecretaris van Financiën [1994] STC 655,* this requirement appears to be incompatible with European Union law.

(*b*) The *consideration for the acquisition* must consist of the *issue of shares* in the acquiring company to all the shareholders of the target company and nothing else except the assumption or discharge of the liabilities of the target company by the acquiring company. For the relief to be available it will be necessary therefore for each shareholder in the target to receive a share in the acquiring company and for there to be no cash element in the consideration paid by the acquiring company.

(*c*) The acquisition must be effected for bona fide commercial reasons and should not form part of a tax avoidance scheme. If clearance has been granted by the Inland Revenue under *Taxation of Chargeable Gains Act 1992, ss 138–139,* it is likely that the Commissioners will regard this requirement as satisfied.

(*d*) After the acquisition each shareholder of each of the companies is a shareholder of the other and the proportion of shares of one of the companies held by any shareholder is the same as the proportion of shares of the other company held by that shareholder. It is necessary therefore that the new shares in the acquiring company are allotted to the shareholders in the acquired company in exactly the same proportions as their holdings in the acquired company.

The Stamp Office is normally prepared to accept that this exemption can apply where the reorganisation involves the transfer of a trading subsidiary of the target company to the acquiring company on the basis that the trading subsidiary is the whole or part of the target company's undertaking. Note, however, that the acquiring company must issue shares to the shareholders of the target company and not to the target company itself.

In this situation the target company may be the holding company of a group of companies and the acquiring company will have been formed by the target company for the purpose of acquiring a trading subsidiary of the target company in return for the issue of shares in the acquiring company to the shareholders of the target company. Due to the existence of the subscribers' shares issued by the acquiring company to the target company a precise mirror image of the target company's share structure cannot be achieved in the acquiring company. Technically, therefore, the exemption from stamp duty will not be available due to the failure of the acquiring company to satisfy (*d*) above. It appears that the legislative draftsman did not foresee this problem (which also occurs frequently when exemption is claimed under *FA 1986, s 77*—see 23.4 below). The Stamp Office is normally co-operative in this matter and when the acquiring company is a private company with say, two subscribers' shares, it will often be prepared to ignore the existence of these shares on the de minimis ground. If the acquiring company is a public limited company it will be required to have an allotted share capital of a nominal value of at least £50,000 of which at least one quarter must be paid-up. [*CA 1985, s 117*]. In these cases the Stamp Office is normally prepared to ignore those shares provided they are cancelled very soon after the transaction so as to create a precise mirror image of the target company's share structure.

In this connection it may also happen that the acquiring company offers to acquire all the shares of the other company in exchange for the issue of shares in the acquiring company to the shareholders of the target company. The offer will be conditional on the acquiring company acquiring all the shares in the other company either by all the shareholders accepting the acquiring company's offer or by reason of the acquiring company exercising the statutory right to acquire minority shareholdings. [*CA 1985, ss 428–430F*]. In the event that it becomes necessary to acquire the minority shareholdings under *CA 1985, ss 428–430F* the acquisition of the shares would take place in stages over a period of time. In such cases the Stamp Office is normally reluctant to fail a claim for exemption on this ground. Care should be taken, however, to ensure that at some point in time the share structure of the acquiring company is a precise mirror image of that of the target company e.g. if trading in the acquiring company's shares occurred before the minority shareholdings were acquired the claim for exemption would probably fail.

23.3 UNDERTAKINGS: REDUCED RATE [*FA 1986, s 76*]

A reduced rate of ad valorem duty under the CONVEYANCE OR TRANSFER (28) on sale head of charge can be claimed where one company ('the acquiring company') acquires the whole or part of the undertaking of another ('the target company'). The reduced rate is 50p per £100 or part of £100 of the amount or value of the consideration. [*FA 1986, s 76(4)*]. Unlike *FA 1986, s 75* where exemption from duty is available (see 23.2 above) it is not necessary under *FA 1986, s 76* for there to be a *scheme of reconstruction* of the target company.

The reduced rate of duty is available on an instrument executed for the purposes of or in connection with the transfer of an undertaking or part of an undertaking or the assignment to the acquiring company by a creditor of any 'relevant debts' owed by the target company. A 'relevant debt' is any debt where the assignor is a bank or trade creditor and any other debt which is less than two years old at the date of the instrument.

The relief is subject to the following requirements:

(*a*) the registered office of the acquiring company must be in the UK. Following the decision of the European Court of Justice in *Halliburton Services BV v Staatssecretaris van Financiën [1994] STC 655,* this requirement appears to be incompatible with European Union law; and

(*b*) the *consideration for the acquisition* must consist of or include the *issue of shares* in the acquiring company to the target company or to all or any of its shareholders and nothing else except cash not exceeding 10% of the nominal value of those shares or the assumption or discharge of the liabilities of the target company by the acquiring company. Unlike *FA 1986, s 75*, there is no requirement that each shareholder in the target receive a share in the acquiring company and there is no bar on including a cash element in the consideration paid by the acquiring company. In relation to the cash element of the consideration the offer will normally be looked at as a whole. In a case concerning the avoidance of CAPITAL DUTY (18)(abolished by *FA 1988*) but relevant for this purpose, Guinness wished to acquire the entire issued share capital in Distillers. The offer document was carefully worded and included a mandate permitting certain Guinness controlled individuals to deal with the form under which the transfer of the Distillers shares would take place in any way they thought fit. By means of a split between stocks and shares in its offer and part payments in cash, Guinness argued that it had satisfied the requirement that the payment of cash 'should not exceed 10% of the nominal value of the shares which made up the balance of the consideration'. The consideration of shares and cash payable to Distillers shareholders was apportionable between the separate blocks of Distillers shares and not to be looked at a whole, argued Guinness. However, the Inland Revenue argued successfully that the offer should be looked at as a whole.

It was held that the offer was an indivisible contract: 'a single offer to take all the accepting shareholders' shares for one consideration comprising stock units and cash, save to the extent that the acceptors exercised one of the options set out in the offer document'. The offer was not altered by including the mandate; the contract remained a contract to acquire all the accepting shareholders' shares for the consideration set down in the offer document. As a result, the cash element exceeded 10% of the nominal value of the shares which made up the balance of the consideration. (*Guinness plc v CIR, [1994] STC 86*).

[*FA 1986, s 76(3)(a)(b)*].

23.4 ACQUISITION OF TARGET COMPANY [*FA 1986, s 77*]

Exemption from stamp duty under the CONVEYANCE OR TRANSFER (28) on sale head of charge is available where a new holding company is placed above an existing company. The exemption applies to an instrument transferring shares in one company (the 'target company') to another company (the 'acquiring company') but is so restricted that it is likely to be of limited use.

The following requirements have to be met.

(*a*) The registered office of the acquiring company must be in the UK. Following the decision of the European Court of Justice in *Halliburton Services BV v Staatssecretaris van Financiën [1994] STC 655,* this requirement appears to be incompatible with European Union law.

(*b*) The transfer of shares must be part of an arrangement under which the acquiring company acquires all the issued shares of the target company. The relief is unlikely to be available, therefore, where the acquiring company already holds shares in the target.

(c) The acquisition must be effected for bona fide commercial reasons and should not form part of a tax avoidance scheme. If clearance has been granted by the Inland Revenue under *Taxation of Chargeable Gains Act 1992, ss 138–139* it is likely that the Commissioners will regard this requirement as satisfied.

(d) The *consideration for the acquisition* must consist only of the *issue of shares* in the acquiring company to the shareholders of the target company. Unlike *FA 1986, ss 75, 76* liabilities undertaken or discharged by the acquiring company are not ignored. Unlike *FA 1986, s 76* there can be no cash element in the consideration paid by the acquiring company.

(e) After the acquisition each person who immediately before it was a shareholder of the target is a shareholder of the acquiring company.

(f) After the acquisition the shares in the acquiring company are of the same classes as were shares in the target immediately before the acquisition. It is understood that a change in the coupon attaching to preference shares or a change in the nominal value of shares of the same class is not regarded by the Commissioners as a reason to refuse the exemption under this requirement or the following two requirements.

(g) After the acquisition the number of shares of any particular class in the acquiring company bears to all the shares in the acquiring company the same proportion as the number of shares of that class in the target company bore to all the shares in the target company immediately before the acquisition.

(h) After the acquisition, the proportion of shares of any particular class in the acquiring company held by any particular shareholder is the same as the proportion of shares of that class in the target company held by him immediately before the acquisition.

It will be apparent from the above requirements that for the exemption to be available at all it will be necessary for the acquiring company following the acquisition to have a share capital which is identical to that of the target.

It is understood that the inclusion of 'stock' in the meaning of 'shares' and 'share capital' by *FA 1986, s 77(4)* was not intended to make debentures and other forms of funded debt subject to the above requirements as strictly required by *FA 1986, s 114(4)* and *SA, s 122(1)*, and that in practice the Commissioners may ignore this unintended result.

23.5 GENERAL INTERPRETATION

(a) '*Consideration for the acquisition*' includes consideration warranted by the transferee company, even if it does not move from that company (*Central & District Properties v CIR HL, [1966] 2 All ER 433*). The consideration for the acquisition does not consist of not less than 90% in shares if those shares are subject to a contract to sell or an option to sell or an option to purchase imposed by the transferee company (*Crane Fruehauf Ltd v CIR CA, [1975] 1 All ER 429*). However, the fact that the consideration shares are issued to the target company which then immediately sells the shares for cash to its holding company does not mean that the acquiring company has in reality provided cash consideration. Accordingly, the acquiring company will not be deprived of the exemption on the ground that the consideration for the acquisition failed to consist as to 90% of the issue of shares by the acquiring company (*CIR v Kent Process Control Ltd [1989] STC 245*). These cases were decided under the now repealed *FA 1927, s 55* but may be relevant to the legislation contained in *FA 1986, ss 75–77* in appropriate cases.

(*b*) '*Issue of shares*' means allotment *and* registration (*Tillotson v CIR CA, [1933] 1 KB 134; National Westminster Bank plc and another v CIR, [1994] 3 All ER 1*). A renounceable letter of allotment is not sufficient. Shares must be issued to the registered holders of shares in an existing company or to the existing company; issue to new nominees or to beneficial owners where nominees are the registered holders is unacceptable (*Brotex Cellulose Fibres v CIR KB, [1933] 1 KB 158; Murex v CIR KB, [1933] 1 KB 173*). Where consideration shares are issued to a target company which then immediately sells the shares for cash to its holding company, it is not correct for the Stamp Office to argue that the consideration shares are not in reality issued to the target company because the holding company could compel the transfer by virtue of its control of the target company in the absence of a formal agreement to that effect. Accordingly, relief will not be refused on this ground unless a requirement to transfer the consideration shares to the holding company is imposed on the target company by the acquiring company (*CIR v Kent Process Control Ltd [1989] STC 245*).

23.6 ADJUDICATION (2)

This is required where exemption or relief is claimed under *FA 1986, ss 75–77*. The claim is made by a letter. The Commissioners have issued specimen letters of claim and notes for guidance which are reproduced in 79 PRACTICAL MATERIALS.

24 Compulsory Purchase

24.1 GENERAL

Where by virtue of any Act of Parliament either

(*a*) property is vested by way of sale in any person, or

(*b*) any person is authorised to purchase property,

the person must produce to the Commissioners, duly stamped with ad valorem duty as a conveyance on sale (see 28 CONVEYANCE OR TRANSFER), a Queen's Printer's copy of the Act or an instrument relating to the vesting in the case of (*a*) or an instrument of conveyance in the case of (*b*). Production must be made within three months of the passing of the Act or the date of vesting, whichever is the later, in the case of (*a*) and completion of the purchase in the case of (*b*). [*FA 1895, s 12*]. A certificate that *FA 1895, s 12* has been complied with is then given on each instrument. For the application of the section to nationalisation schemes, see 24.4 below.

This provision does not require that a conveyance be taken of goods, wares or merchandise forming part of the property. If the acquisition relates exclusively to goods etc. no instrument need be produced to the Commissioners. [*FA 1949, s 36(4)*]. If the conveyance does include goods etc. ad valorem duty will be payable on the attributable compensation moneys.

24.2 CONSIDERATION/COMPENSATION MONEYS

Ad valorem duty will be paid on the consideration for the transaction and reference should be made generally to 25 CONSIDERATION. See 24.3 below for consideration for the compulsory purchase of land. See 24.1 above for consideration attributable to goods etc.

24.3 COMPULSORY PURCHASE OF LAND

(*a*) A general vesting declaration under *Compulsory Purchase (Vesting Declarations) Act 1981* under which a local authority acquires land compulsorily may cover more than one property but will nevertheless be regarded as a separate transaction for each property with the consequence that a CERTIFICATE OF VALUE (19) can be given in respect of each transaction where appropriate.

(*b*) A compulsory purchase effected by deed poll bears duty as a conveyance on sale to the acquiring authority. [*Compulsory Purchase Act 1965, s 28(2)*]. See also *Lands Clauses Consolidation Act 1845, s 77* (as amended by *Administration of Justice Act 1965, ss 17, 18* and *Compulsory Purchase Act 1965, s 39*); *Acquisition of Land Act 1981*.

(*c*) Duty is charged on the total compensation moneys payable in respect of the sale of land including any part representing compensation for severance relating to land not transferred (*Law Society's Gazette 1953 p 206*). Compensation for loss of business may be included as consideration for the sale of land (*Glasgow & South Western Rly Co v CIR HL, (1887) 12 App Cas 315*).

(*d*) Compensation moneys may be undetermined at the date of acquisition and the following is the practice relating to the charging of stamp duty.

  (i) wholly determined—ad valorem duty on the compensation moneys; a CERTIFICATE OF VALUE (19) may be given;

  (ii) partly determined—ad valorem duty on the ascertained part and 50p miscellaneous conveyance duty on the remainder; a CERTIFICATE OF VALUE (19) cannot be given;

(iii) wholly undetermined—50p miscellaneous conveyance duty; a CERTIFICATE OF VALUE (19) cannot be given.

(*e*) A declaration is a conveyance on sale and so must be produced under *FA 1931, s 28* (see 66 PRODUCED STAMP).

24.4 NATIONALISATION

The rules set out in 24.1 above are modified in the case of nationalisation schemes so that

(*a*) in computing duty under *FA 1895, s 12* (see 24.1 above) the consideration is left out of account, and

(*b*) no stamp duty is payable on any conveyance, agreement or assignment or other instrument made solely for the purpose of effecting a transfer.

A nationalisation scheme to which this exemption applies is one effected by an Act embodying a scheme for the carrying on of the whole or part of an industry or an undertaking under national ownership or control. The exemption extends to transfers made to the Crown or a specially constituted body as part of the initial putting into force of the scheme. [*FA 1946, s 52*].

24.5 Generally the Acts enabling the creation, dissolution or reorganisation of a nationalised industry or other government organisation contain special provisions relating to exemption from stamp duty; nationalised industries etc. are not exempt without special provision. Most commonly the Acts provide that *FA 1895, s 12* (see 24.1 above) shall not apply, but other provisions exempting certain instruments are sometimes included (e.g. exemption for shares in nationalised companies—*FA 1948, s 74*).

25   Consideration

25.1 Ad valorem duty on a CONVEYANCE OR TRANSFER (28) on sale is normally charged by reference to the amount or value of the consideration. However, for instruments executed on or after 8 December 1993 relating to interests in land the market value of the property conveyed or transferred may be used to calculate the stamp duty charge when the consideration cannot be ascertained at the time of sale (see 25.9 below).

Exemption is available if the instrument contains a CERTIFICATE OF VALUE (19) that the amount or value of the consideration does not exceed £60,000. The following paragraphs explain the way in which the amount or value of the consideration is calculated or the stamp duty charge is otherwise calculated.

25.2 CASH

Where sterling constitutes the consideration for sale no problem generally arises (but see 25.4 below).

If the consideration is expressed in a foreign currency the currency is converted at the rate of exchange at the date of the instrument. If the instrument contains a statement of the rate of exchange, the instrument will be deemed duly stamped in accordance with that statement unless and until it is shown that the statement is untrue and the instrument is insufficiently stamped. [*SA, s 6*]. *FA 1985, s 88* ended the system of converting various specified currencies at fixed rates published from time to time in the London Gazette.

25.3 STOCK (INCLUDING SHARES) AND SECURITIES

(*a*) **Stock and marketable securities**
The value of stock or marketable securities is taken into account. [*SA, s 55(1)*]. This value is calculated according to the average price of the stock or security; an instrument containing a statement of the average price and stamped in accordance with that statement is deemed duly stamped unless and until it is shown that the statement is untrue and the instrument is insufficiently stamped. [*SA, s 6*].

(i) **Listed stock or securities** are in practice valued at the value used for capital gains tax purposes which is usually the lower of

(A) the lower of the two prices shown in The Stock Exchange Daily Official List plus one-quarter of the difference between the two prices, and

(B) halfway between the highest and lowest prices at which bargains were recorded on that day (ignoring special bargains).

[*Taxation of Chargeable Gains Act 1992, s 272(3)*].

(ii) **Unlisted shares or marketable securities** will be valued on a net assets, earnings or yield basis as appropriate. They may be valued by reference to the value of the property for which they form the consideration (e.g. *Foster (John) & Sons Ltd v CIR CA, [1894] 1 QB 516; Carlyon Estate Ltd v CIR KB, (1937) 46 TC 413*).

(*b*) **Unmarketable securities,** e.g. some debentures in private companies, are valued at the principal amount outstanding plus accrued interest at the date of the conveyance. [*SA, s 55(2)*].

25.4 PERIODICAL PAYMENTS

Where the consideration consists of periodical payments (e.g. an annuity, payments by instalments), amounts are charged to ad valorem duty as follows:

(*a*) payable periodically for a definite period not exceeding 20 years—the total of the payments;

(*b*) payable periodically for a definite period exceeding 20 years or in perpetuity or for an indefinite period (not terminable with life)—the total amount which will or may, according to the terms of sale, be payable during 20 years from the date of the instrument;

(*c*) payable periodically for a life or lives—the total amount which will or may, according to the terms of sale, be payable during twelve years from the date of the instrument.

[*SA, s 56; FA 1971, s 69, 14 Sch, Part VI*].

The periodic payments charged are those which form a part of the sale transaction and not those which are an inherent part of the property. Thus, rent payments under a leasehold would not be chargeable, but the reservation of a rent charge would. Contingent payments are chargeable, for example, on a company achieving a certain level of profits (*Underground Electric Rlys Co of London Ltd v CIR HL, [1906] AC 21*); and see 26 CONTINGENCY PRINCIPLE. Sums which can only become payable on breach of the sale contract are not taken into account (*Western United Investment Co Ltd v CIR Ch D, [1958] Ch 392*). The Court of Appeal considered the application of (*b*) above in *Blendett v CIR* and *Quietlece v CIR CA, [1984] STC 95* (heard together). In the *Blendett* case a company was granted a lease for a premium of £240,500 payable as to £50,000 on execution and as to the balance on the 23rd anniversary of the lease. In the *Quietlece* case a company was granted a lease for a premium of £370,900 payable as to £50,000 on execution and as to the balance in three equal yearly instalments commencing on the 23rd anniversary of the lease. Ad valorem duty was paid in both cases only on the initial payments of £50,000 and the companies argued that the premiums were payable periodically for a period exceeding 20 years within (*b*) above and therefore duty was payable only on the consideration paid in the first 20 years. The Court held in the *Blendett* case that two payments only, made more than 20 years apart, were not periodical payments. In the *Quietlece* case it was held that the instalments were not 'payable periodically for a definite period' because there was only one payment during the first 20 years.

In both cases the Court held that (*b*) above did not apply and accordingly ad valorem duty was payable on the total premium paid by each company.

25.5 DEBTS AND LIABILITIES

Where property is conveyed

(*a*) for consideration consisting wholly or in part of a debt due to the transferee, or

(*b*) subject to the payment or transfer of money or stock, whether or not charged on the property and whether or not contingent,

the debt, money or stock is deemed to be the consideration. [*SA, s 57*].

The amount of the debt is to be taken into account notwithstanding that the debt may be considered to be bad or doubtful and therefore worth less commercially. However, if the application of *SA, s 57* results in a consideration which would exceed the value of the property conveyed, the consideration is limited to that value provided that the instrument is adjudicated (see 2 ADJUDICATION). [*FA 1980, s 102*].

Foreclosure orders are subject to special rules (see 45 FORECLOSURE). For the ascertainment of an amount contingently payable see 26 CONTINGENCY PRINCIPLE.

The conveyance of property subject to a mortgage will be charged to ad valorem duty on the consideration including the amount outstanding on the mortgage (e.g. *City of Glasgow Bank (Liquidators) CS, (1881) 8 R(Ct of Sess) 389*).

The Commissioners have published a Statement of Practice (SP 6/90) on conveyances and transfers of property subject to a debt. The text of this Statement and the accompanying press release is as follows:

'The Inland Revenue have published today a Statement of Practice (SP 6/90) concerning stamp duty on a conveyance or transfer where property is subject to a mortgage or other debt. A copy of the Statement is attached.

Scope of the Statement

The Statement relates to conveyances or transfers where

— the transferee takes over liability for the whole or part of the debt

   and

— there is no other consideration for the transfer (in particular, no monetary payment).

Situations where the Statement may apply include

— transfers of mortgaged property between spouses, including into or out of joint names

— transfers within a family of mortgaged business property, for example farmland.

Since the duty on gifts was abolished in 1985, there have been a number of enquiries and misunderstandings about the correct stamp duty treatment of such transfers. The Statement is being issued to clarify the Department's view of the law.

Effect

Broadly, the Statement records the Inland Revenue's view that certain transfers of mortgaged property where no money passes are nonetheless sales for stamp duty purposes. These are transfers where

(i) the transferee makes an express covenant (in the form, for example, of a specific undertaking to the lender at the time of the transfer), either to pay part or all of the mortgage debt, or to indemnify the transferor against his personal liability to the lender;

or

(ii) a covenant by the transferee in similar terms is (except in Scotland) implied by law and no contrary intention is established.

Such transfers of property are sales and subject to the stamp duty charge under the 'Conveyance or Transfer on sale' head. The duty payable is 1 per cent of the debt taken over by the transferee.

NOTES FOR EDITORS

1. Where property is conveyed or transferred subject to a debt (e.g. a house or flat on which there is a mortgage), the stamp duty payable on the sale reflects any part of the debt taken over by the transferee (Section 57, Stamp Act 1891). If there is no cash element, the debt taken over will account for the whole of the chargeable consideration on which the duty is calculated.

Transfers between Spouses

2. The Statement of Practice explains that, for example, where a mortgaged property held in the name of one spouse is transferred into the joint names of both spouses, the transferee acquiring a half share in the property may be regarded as taking over the obligation to discharge one-half of the outstanding mortgage. Where that is so, the assumption of part of the debt will constitute consideration for the share acquired in the property and for stamp duty purposes the transaction is not a gift but a sale.

Separation and Divorce

3. On the other hand, the Statement also explains that, in certain circumstances, where a share in the marital home, or the whole of it, is transferred subject to a mortgage from one partner of the marriage to the other as part of the arrangements for their separation or divorce, such a conveyance or transfer may be exempted from ad valorem duty (even if it would otherwise be chargeable for reasons explained above).

STAMP DUTY

CONVEYANCES AND TRANSFERS OF PROPERTY SUBJECT TO A DEBT—SECTION 57 STAMP ACT 1891

Introduction

1. Since the abolition of the duty on voluntary dispositions in 1985, many enquiries have been received about the stamp duty chargeable on conveyances etc. subject to a debt where *no* chargeable consideration (e.g. money or stock) unrelated to the debt is given by the transferee. This Statement of Practice sets out the Board's view of the correct stamp duty treatment of such conveyances.

25.5 Consideration

2. For the sake of completeness it should be noted that where chargeable consideration unrelated to debt *is* given by the transferee, Section 57 renders the conveyance liable to ad valorem duty on the aggregate of that consideration and the debt whether the transferee assumes liability for the debt or not (*IRC v City of Glasgow Bank 1881 8 R389, 18 SLR 242*).

Section 57, Stamp Act 1891

3. The most commonly misunderstood applications of Section 57 arise where

   — a mortgaged property held in the name of the spouse is transferred into the joint names of both spouses;

   — a mortgaged property held in the name of one spouse or in their joint names is transferred into the sole name of the other;

   — a mortgaged business property, frequently farmland, is conveyed from a sole proprietor to a family partnership or from a family partnership to a fresh partnership bringing in other members of the family.

4. The critical question is whether the transaction to which the conveyance gives effect is or is not a sale. If it is, Section 57 will apply and the conveyance will be chargeable to ad valorem duty on the amount of the debt assumed. If it is not, then Section 57 will not apply and ad valorem duty will not be payable.

Express Covenants

5. Where property is transferred subject to a debt, the transferee may covenant, either in the instrument or by means of a separate written undertaking, to pay the debt or indemnify the transferor against his personal liability to the lender. Such a covenant or undertaking constitutes valuable consideration and, in view of Section 57, establishes the transaction as a sale for stamp duty purposes.

6. Where the transferor covenants to pay the debt and the transferee does not assume any liability for it, no chargeable consideration has been given and there is no sale. The transfer would then be a voluntary disposition—i.e. an unencumbered gift capable of being certified as Category L under the Stamp Duty (Exempt Instruments) Regulations 1987 (SI 1987 No 516)—and so exempt from the 50p charge that would otherwise arise.

Implied Covenants

7. Where no express covenant or undertaking is given by the transferee, the Board are advised that, except in Scotland, a covenant by the transferee may be implied. That makes the transaction a sale, as in paragraph 4 above.

8.   Such an implied covenant may be negated if there is evidence that it was the intention of the parties at the time of the transfer that the transferor should continue to be liable for the whole of the mortgage debt. Where evidence of such a contrary intention exists, the transfer would again be treated for stamp duty purposes as a voluntary disposition.

9.   Where property in joint names subject to a debt is transferred to one of the joint holders (though with no cash passing), a covenant by the transferee to indemnify the transferor may be implied even where both parties were jointly liable on the mortgage.

Amount Chargeable

10. Where a conveyance of property subject to a debt is chargeable to ad valorem duty and the express or implied covenant by the transferee relates only to part of the debt, only the amount of that part is treated as chargeable consideration within Section 57. A certificate of value under Section 34(4) Finance Act 1958 may, where appropriate, be included in the conveyance where the relevant amount of the debt does not exceed the amount certified.

Other Provisions

11. The foregoing does not affect any statutory exemption from duty that may apply, e.g. that for transfers to a charity (Section 129 Finance Act 1982) and that available for certain transfers of property from one party to a marriage to the other in connection with their divorce or separation (Section 83(1) Finance Act 1985 and Category H of the Stamp Duty (Exempt Instruments) Regulations 1987).

Procedure

12. Where the applicant is satisfied that the conveyance or transfer is made on sale, it may be sent or taken for stamping with a remittance for the duty payable. If the transfer contains an appropriate certificate of value—see paragraph 10 above—it may be sent direct to the Land Registry in the usual way if appropriate. In either case, if the amount of the debt outstanding is not given in the conveyance or transfer the amount should be stated in a covering letter.

13. Where the conveyance or transfer contains a covenant by the transferor to pay the debt (see paragraph 6) and is certified as within category L of the Stamp Duty (Exempt Instruments) Regulations 1987, it should also be sent direct to the Land Registry if appropriate.

14.   In any other case where the applicant believes that the conveyance or transfer effects a voluntary disposition—see paragraph 8 above—it should be presented for adjudication accompanied by a statement of the facts and any supporting evidence.'

It is thought that the views expressed by the Commissioners in the above Statement of Practice are incorrect in the context of matrimonial and family relationships where there will usually be no question of any intention to enter legal relations and hence there will be no contract between the transferor and the transferee. If there is no contract there will be no sale and no ad valorem duty will be chargeable. For example, where one spouse transfers the domestic home into the joint names of both spouses it will be a requirement of the mortgagee that both spouses share equal responsibility for the mortgage debt. However, it would be wrong to treat the transaction as a sale contract between the spouses where the transfer has been made either simply in order that both spouses own the home or for tax planning reasons. This may become an issue with the advent of independent taxation of husband and wife. Similarly, it is thought that ad valorem duty is not chargeable under *SA, s 57* where mortgaged business property such as farmland is transferred from a sole proprietor to his family partnership. The desire of a father or mother to bring their children into the family business by gift is not a sale despite the incidental assumption of liabilities by the newly introduced partners, and so no ad valorem duty is chargeable. Curiously, paragraph 4 of the text of the Statement of Practice appears to recognise this although the overall thrust of the Statement of Practice appears to be that *SA, s 57* turns the transaction into a sale rather than *SA, s 57* depending for its application on the transaction first being properly analysed as a sale.

An agreement to settle trade or other liabilities as part of the consideration for the sale of a business will cause the amount of those liabilities to be added to the consideration (*E Gomme Ltd v CIR Ch D, [1964] 3 All ER 497*); but it is possible to provide for the settlement of liabilities by the vendor out of the realisation of the monetary assets without the purchaser's undertaking to find any deficiency, in which case duty may be saved.

Liabilities inherent in the property (e.g. future calls on partly-paid shares, rent under a lease) are not treated as part of the consideration (*Swayne v CIR CA, [1900] 1 QB 172*).

25.6   COVENANTS TO IMPROVE PROPERTY

A conveyance on sale made for any consideration chargeable to ad valorem duty is not liable to duty in respect of any further consideration consisting of a covenant by the purchaser to make substantial improvements or additions to the property conveyed (or in consideration of his having done so) or a covenant relating to the subject matter of the conveyance. [*FA 1900, s 10*]. This section was held to apply to a contract for the sale of land and a separate contract (conditional on the first) for the vendor to build a house for the purchaser so that ad valorem duty was charged only on the consideration for the first contract (*Kimbers & Co v CIR KB, [1936] 1 KB 132; Paul v CIR CS (1936), SC 443*; cf. *McInnes v CIR CS (1934), SC 424*).

Following their defeat in the case of *Prudential Assurance Co Ltd v CIR [1992] BTC 8,094* the Inland Revenue have issued a new Statement of Practice (SP8/93) to supersede those issued in 1957 and 1987 (SP10/87).

The facts of the case were that Prudential agreed to purchase freehold land including unfinished buildings from developers. Three documents were executed simultaneously. The first document was a sale agreement by which Prudential agreed to purchase the property for £2.5m. The second document was a development agreement by which the developers were to execute existing building contracts and Prudential were to provide the required moneys up to an agreed maximum on a monthly basis after taking into account the £2.5m payable under the sale agreement. The third document was a transfer of the land to Prudential. The question was whether the transfer was stampable on the £2.5m sale price plus the cost of building work already completed (total £6m) or on the total amount payable for the land and the cost of all building work (total £10.7m). It was held that although all three documents were part of one transaction, the sale agreement was, as the parties had intended, completed independently of the carrying out of the remaining building works under the development agreement. The transfer was therefore properly stampable on £6m and not £10.7m.

SP 8/93 applies where

(*a*) there is a contract for the sale or lease of a building plot and the builder or developer is to construct buildings on the site for the purchaser; and

(*b*) at the date of the contract, building work on the plot has either not been started or is incomplete; and

(*c*) at the time of the conveyance or execution of the lease, building work on the plot has begun (or has been completed).

Whilst each case will depend on its own facts, in broad terms the treatment will be as follows:

(i) Where there is a contract for a conveyance or lease of land, and, as a separate transaction, a further contract for building works to be carried out, stamp duty on the conveyance or lease will be calculated without regard to the further contract.

(ii) Where, within a single transaction, there are separate contracts for the sale or lease of land, and for building works on the land, the stamp duty charge depends on whether the contracts are genuinely independent. If the contracts are independent, duty is charged on the price paid or payable for both the land itself and for any building that is on the land at the time the instrument is executed, including partly completed buildings. If the contracts are not genuinely independent, stamp duty will be charged on the total price for the land and completed buildings.

The statement will not apply where there is evidence of a sham or artificial transaction.

The Statement of Practice does not affect the common situation where a contract for the sale of a new house on a plot of land is subsequently given effect by a conveyance of the whole property, in the same way as most ordinary sales of new houses.

If stamp duty is offered on the total price paid for the building plot and the completed buildings, the documents should be submitted to the Stamp Office in the usual way. If the total price does not exceed the £60,000 threshold (see 19 CERTIFICATE OF VALUE), the documents can be sent direct to the Land Registry under the *Stamp Duty (Exempt Instruments) Regulations 1985*. Where the total price paid exceeds the threshold and the purchaser contends that the duty is payable on a lesser sum than the total price, the Board have requested that the documents should be sent to the Stamp Office together with a full explanation.

25.7 EXCHANGES OF PROPERTY

Prior to *FA 1994, s 241* duty under the head CONVEYANCE OR TRANSFER (28) on sale was only charged where there was a 'sale' for stamp duty purposes. Basically, this meant that there had to be a transfer of property in consideration of stock, marketable securities or debt.

An exchange of property is not a 'sale' for stamp duty purposes and therefore sale duty was not charged except in the case of an exchange of one freehold property for another and even then sale duty was only charged by reference to any equality money, under *SA, s 73*. On any other exchange of property including freehold for leasehold property, *SA, s 73* did not apply and the Inland Revenue seemed to accept that the payment of equality money did not make the exchange a 'sale' for stamp duty purposes.

As a result of the exploitation of this rule involving the transfer of a freehold property in exchange for a lease of low value plus equality money equal to the balance of the price the position has been altered by *FA 1994, s 241*.

As a consequence, where the consideration for the transfer or vesting of any estate or interest in land or the grant of LEASE (53) or tack consists of or includes any property (which would not previously have been taken into account), then the market value of that property is to be taken as the consideration (or part thereof) for the purposes of charging sale duty.

25.8 However, there are some difficulties with the drafting and operation of *FA 1994, s 241*. By far the most serious difficulty relates to the amount of sale duty to be charged on an exchange. In the November 1993 Budget the Inland Revenue at first maintained that an exchange of properties of unequal value with equality money would have to be stamped on both legs of the exchange on the full value of the most expensive property e.g. on an exchange of property A worth £150,000 for property B worth £100,000 plus £50,000 cash, duty would be charged on both transfers by reference to £150,000 on the basis that the consideration for property B was property A.

However, in their Press Release of 18 April 1994 the Inland Revenue revised this to state that, 'where it is clear from the contract that the intention of the parties to the transaction is that the cheaper property should be transferred for the more expensive property *less* the equality money, the Stamp Office will limit the charge to duty accordingly'. Therefore in the above example duty would be charged on the transfer of property B by reference to £100,000 and not £150,000.

In the same Press Release the Inland Revenue somewhat surprisingly went on at paragraph 12 to explain how *FA 1994, s 241* could be avoided and sale duty saved on one leg of the exchange. In many cases, transactions which could normally be structured and documented as exchanges can equally well be carried out as sales for a price which is partly satisfied in kind. To achieve this result, a single contract should provide for a sale of the more expensive property (A) in consideration of the transfer of the cheaper property (B) plus the cash. To assist the calculation of duty, the single contract should state the values which the parties place on A and B. The parties should be referred to as Seller and Buyer and should agree in advance who will pay the duty. The single contract should be completed by two transfers. The transfer of A, being on the sale of A attracts sale duty of 1% of the consideration i.e. the value of B plus the cash. The transfer of B attracts only the fixed 50p duty because this transfer is not on sale but is merely the means whereby part of the consideration for the sale of A is vested in the seller. The transfer of A should be expressed as 'being in consideration of the transfer of B and the payment of £. . .'. The transfer of B should be expressed as being 'pursuant to the terms of the Agreement for Sale dated . . .'.

One of the solicitors should submit both transfers for adjudication plus a copy of the contract, although this is not compulsory. The transfer of A will need to be produced under *FA 1931, s 28* (see 66 PRODUCED STAMP).

ADJUDICATION (2) is recommended to protect against the possibility of a third party or a defendant in future legal proceedings raising a stamp objection by arguing that the transfer of B is insufficiently stamped.

See 28.9 CONVEYANCE OR TRANSFER in relation to sub-sales.

25.9 UNASCERTAINED AND CONTINGENT CONSIDERATION

See also 26 CONTINGENCY PRINCIPLE.

In addition to the matters described in 25.8 above, *FA 1994* also set out to change another basic stamp duty principle. That principle was that if the consideration for a sale was unascertainable at the date of the instrument, no ad valorem duty could be charged. This was always subject to the CONTINGENCY PRINCIPLE (26) which holds that where the consideration payable under an instrument is uncertain and dependent on a contingency, but a maximum, minimum or basic figure can be ascertained then ad valorem duty is payable by reference to that figure regardless of the fact that such figure may not ultimately be paid.

FA 1994, s 242 alters this basic principle in relation to interests in land by charging ad valorem duty on the market value of the property transferred where all or part of the consideration is unascertainable and the CONTINGENCY PRINCIPLE (26) does not apply (because there is no prima facie figure).

As with *FA 1994, s 241* (see 25.8 above) there are some difficulties with the drafting and operation of *Sec 242*. It is clear that *Sec 242* is intended to introduce an ad valorem charge in situations where the consideration takes the form of a right to a future payment which is unascertainable at the date of the instrument and there is no maximum, minimum or prima facie sum for the CONTINGENCY PRINCIPLE (26) to operate on. However, it is also clear from the decision in *Marren v Ingles HL, [1980] STC 500* that a right to a future payment is a form of property, being a chose in action. On the basis that that right is property for the purposes of *Sec 241*, does *Sec 241* override *Sec 242* and charge ad valorem duty on the market value of that right on the basis that the value of that right (property) has been ascertained? Indeed, it is arguable that *Sec 242* has no effect because it is either overridden by *Sec 241* or the CONTINGENCY PRINCIPLE (26). However, it is thought that a court would be reluctant to hold that *Sec 242* has no function and would probably conclude that a right to a future payment is not property for the purpose of *Sec 241* thereby allowing *Sec 242* to operate.

Also, it is unclear as to whether the intention that *FA 1994, s 242* should not apply where the CONTINGENCY PRINCIPLE (26) operates has been achieved. *FA 1994, s 242(3)(a)* excludes from the effect of *Sec 242* cases where the consideration or rent could be ascertained on the assumption that a future event mentioned in the instrument were or were not to occur. However, the CONTINGENCY PRINCIPLE (26) is wider than this and operates even when there is no express mention of an event in the instrument. For example, on the grant of a lease where the rent could later increase by reason of the exercise of the option to tax the rent for VAT purposes, the Stamp Office charges duty on the rent on the basis that the option to tax has been exercised (see 78 VAT AND STAMP DUTY). Clearly, there will be leases which contain no reference to the option to tax for VAT purposes. Does this result in *Sec 242* applying to the exclusion of the CONTINGENCY PRINCIPLE (26) on the basis that no relevant event is mentioned in the instrument and so stamp duty must be charged on the market rent i.e. the actual rent and not the rent as increased by the notional VAT charge?

FA 1994, s 242 applies where the consideration, or any part of the consideration, for the transfer or vesting of any estate or interest in land or the grant of any lease or tack cannot be ascertained at the time the instrument is executed and the CONTINGENCY PRINCIPLE (26) does not apply. The consideration is then taken to be the market value of the estate or interest or lease or tack immediately before the instrument is executed ad valorem duty is charged on such value. In relation to duty chargeable on rent under the heading 'lease or tack' in *SA, 1 Sch*, the rent or any part of the rent cannot be ascertained, the rent is taken to be the market rent at the time the lease is executed.

Where *FA 1994, s 242* applies it will be necessary to carry out a valuation of the property concerned.

25.10 MISCELLANEOUS

(*a*) Interest on the purchase price is not included in the amount of the consideration on which duty is charged (*Hotung v Collector of Stamp Revenue PC, [1965] AC 766*).

(*b*) If the purchaser undertakes to bear the vendor's legal costs, this will normally form part of the consideration. In practice this does not generally extend to a lessee's undertaking to bear the lessor's costs.

25.11 VALUE ADDED TAX

For the calculation of stamp duty where the consideration includes or may include value added tax see 25.9 above and 78 VAT AND STAMP DUTIES.

26 Contingency Principle

26.1 The amount of consideration chargeable to ad valorem duty is the amount ascertainable at the date of the execution of the instrument (see e.g. *Underground Electric Rlys Co of London Ltd v CIR HL, [1906] AC 21*). While the instrument should contain all the facts and circumstances affecting the liability to duty and the amount of the duty [*SA, s 5*], there may often be circumstances where the amount of the consideration itself cannot be stated in the instrument.

26.2 Where the consideration payable under an instrument is uncertain and dependent on the happening of a contingency, the contingency principle applies as follows.

(*a*) Where the maximum amount which will be payable on the happening of the contingency can be ascertained, duty is payable on the maximum (*Underground Electric Rlys Co of London Ltd v CIR CA, [1916] 1 KB 306; Coventry City Council v CIR Ch D, [1978] 1 All ER 1107*).

(*b*) Where, although the maximum amount which will be payable on the happening of a contingency cannot be ascertained, there is an ascertainable minimum amount, duty is payable on that minimum (*Underground Electric Rlys Co of London Ltd v CIR HL, [1906] AC 21*).

(*c*) Where no maximum or minimum can be ascertained because it is a basic figure subject to increase or reduction by reference to unknown factors, duty is payable by reference to the basic figure (*Independent Television Authority v CIR HL, [1961] AC 427*).

And see 25.9 CONSIDERATION.

26.3 If the consideration is undetermined, but ascertainable at the date of the instrument (e.g. where the consideration is agreed to be ascertained by reference to a valuation or a set of accounts which are not yet available), the duty will be assessed on the amount of the consideration as subsequently ascertained.

26.4 Contingency Principle

26.4 In a case where the consideration is undetermined and unascertainable at the date of the instrument the general rule is that no ad valorem duty is chargeable. For example, where there is no maximum, minimum or basic figure and the consideration is to be determined by a formula which is dependent on some future event taking place. However, in relation to the transfer or vesting of any estate or interest in land or the grant of any lease or tack the position has been changed by *FA 1994, s 242*. In such cases ad valorem duty is charged on instruments executed after 7 December 1993 and the consideration is for this purpose taken to be the market value of estate or interest or lease or tack. See also 25.9 CONSIDERATION.

26.5 It is by no means certain that the contingency principle applies to the CONVEYANCE OR TRANSFER (28) on sale head of charge. The Stamp Office has recently conceded that the contingency principle does not apply where the contingent consideration consists of shares or securities. There appears to be no valid basis for distinguishing shares and cash consideration in this area. Nevertheless, the Stamp Office continues to reject the argument that the contingency principle does not apply to the CONVEYANCE OR TRANSFER (28) on sale head of charge despite the fact that there is no case which specifically applies the principle to that head of charge.

27 Contract Notes

27.1 Contract note duty was abolished by *FA 1985, s 86*. This duty was payable on notes sent by brokers to their clients in respect of the purchase and sale of shares and securities.

27.2 The obligation under *F(1909–10)A 1910* to issue contract notes has also been cancelled. [*FA 1987, s 49*]. Contract notes are still required under the rules of the Securities and Investments Board.

28 Conveyance or Transfer

28.1 There are two heads of charge in relation to Conveyances or Transfers in *SA, 1 Sch* and they cover the following conveyances or transfers.

(*a*) On sale of any property—ad valorem duty (for rates, see 28.3 below). See 28.2 to 28.11 below.

(*b*) Any other kind—fixed duty 50p. See 28.12 below.

28.2 CONVEYANCE OR TRANSFER ON SALE

In addition to being charged on instruments directly operating as conveyances or transfers on sale, ad valorem duty is charged on the following.

(*a*) Certain agreements and contracts for sale—see 6.3 AGREEMENT FOR SALE.

(*b*) Instruments creating and selling ANNUITIES (7).

(*c*) Absolute BILLS OF SALE (15).

(*d*) Instruments charged under *FA 1895, s 12* (see 24 COMPULSORY PURCHASE).

(*e*) FORECLOSURE (45) orders.

(*f*) RELEASE AND RENUNCIATION (69) of property on sale.

For exemptions available in respect of company transactions see 12 ASSOCIATED COMPANIES, 23 COMPANY REORGANISATIONS.

28.3 RATES OF AD VALOREM DUTY

The rates are as follows. [*FA 1963, s 55*].

Property conveyed	Amount or value of consideration	Rate
Stock or marketable securities	Any sum	50p for every £100 or part of £100 of consideration
Other property	Up to £500	50p for every £50 or part of £50 of consideration
Other property as above	Over £500	£1 for every £100 or part of £100 of consideration

Instruments certified at £60,000 or less are exempt from duty under this head. See 19 CERTIFICATE OF VALUE. A certificate of value cannot be given in respect of transfers of stock, marketable securities or unit trust units. The rate is 50p per £100 or part thereof of the consideration. [*FA 1963, s 55(1A)*].

The ad valorem rates applicable to a conveyance or transfer on sale are also used to calculate the duty applicable to

(*a*) premiums on LEASES (53);

(*b*) certain BEARER INSTRUMENTS (13);

28.4 Conveyance or Transfer

(c) equality money on an EXCHANGE OR PARTITION (37);

(d) a company's purchase of its own shares (see 67 PURCHASE OF OWN SHARES).

A special rate of ad valorem duty of £1.50 for every £100 or part of £100 is charged in connection with DEPOSITARY RECEIPTS (34) and CLEARANCE SERVICES (22).

28.4 CONVEYANCE ON SALE

This includes every instrument or decree or order of any court or commissioners whereby any property (or estate or interest therein) on sale is transferred to or vested in a purchaser, or any person on his behalf or on his direction. [*SA, s 54*].

28.5 The following have been held to be conveyances on sale.

(a) A deed executed pursuant to an agreement for the dissolution of a partnership (*Garnett v CIR QB, (1899) 81 LT 633*; cf. *MacLeod v CIR Ex (S) 1885, 22 Sc LR 674*); and see 62 PARTNERSHIPS.

(b) A lease (see *Littlewoods Mail Order Stores Ltd HL 1962, [1963] AC 135*).

(c) An agreement creating an option to purchase land (*George Wimpey & Co Ltd v CIR CA, [1975] 2 All ER 45*). See 59 OPTIONS AND EQUITY WARRANTS.

(d) A declaration of trust in favour of a purchaser (*Chesterfield Brewery Co v CIR QB, [1899] 2 QB 7*).

(e) An incomplete transfer of shares where the transferee and the consideration were not shown (*Fitch Lovell Ltd v CIR Ch D, [1962] 3 All ER 685*).

(f) A receipt for the sale consideration (*Fleetwood-Hesketh v CIR CA, [1963] 1 KB 351*). See 68 RECEIPTS.

The property conveyed need not be the same property as that which was the subject of the sale bargain if the property conveyed represents it but not if its conveyance is merely a consequence of the sale (*Henty and Constable (Brewers) Ltd v CIR CA, [1961] 3 All ER 1146*). A conveyance or transfer will be chargeable as a conveyance or transfer on sale notwithstanding that at the time of execution of the instrument of conveyance or transfer the beneficial interest in the property contracted to be sold has already passed or passes at some time other than that of contract. Examples are conveyances where the purchaser is already the beneficial owner of the property under a prior contract (*Parway Estates Ltd v CIR CA, (1958) 45 TC 135*) and a transfer pursuant to what was at the time a conditional sale agreement (*Ridge Nominees Ltd v CIR CA, [1961] 3 All ER 1108*).

For conveyances in contemplation of sale see 28.11 below.

28.6 **SALE**

'Sale' is not defined in the legislation but will require a vendor, a purchaser, something sold and a price.

Reference should be made to the following sections of this book for transactions which may be treated as sales.

(*a*) ASSENTS (11).

(*b*) EXCHANGE OR PARTITION (37).

(*c*) FAMILY ARRANGEMENTS AND DIVORCE (42).

(*d*) PARTNERSHIPS (62).

(*e*) RECEIPTS (68).

(*f*) RELEASE AND RENUNCIATION (69).

See also *Ridge Nominees Ltd v CIR CA, [1961] 3 All ER 1108* (compulsory acquisition of shares from dissentients under *Companies Act 1985, ss 428–430* liable as a conveyance on sale); *Great Western Rly Co v CIR CA, [1894] 1 QB 507* (amalgamation of two railway companies by transfer of undertakings to a new company and dissolution of transferor companies liable as a sale); *Belch v CIR Ex(S) 1877, 14 Sc LR 389* and *Gibb v CIR Ex(S) 1880, 18 Sc LR 477* (exercise of right of repurchase or extinction of an interest which was created by the document giving the right not liable as a sale).

28.7 **PROPERTY**

For a conveyance or transfer to be liable it must relate to property. 'Property' is not defined in the legislation, but includes anything which belongs to one person exclusive of others and which can be made the subject-matter of bargain and sale to another (*Potter v CIR Ex, (1854) 10 Ex 147*). A right which a company did not in law possess (the exclusive right to use the company's asphalt in certain areas) was not property and could not, therefore, be conveyed or transferred (*Limmer Asphalte Paving Co v CIR Ex, (1872) LR 7 Ex 211*).

The following, inter alia, are property.

(*a*) Land.

(*b*) Personalty—many forms of personal property may be transferred by delivery and need not attract ad valorem duty unless incorporated in an instrument of transfer.

(*c*) Stock and marketable securities—instruments of transfer are required for transfers of shares and debentures [*Companies Act 1985, s 183(1)*] and unit trusts [*FA 1946, s 56(4)*].

(*d*) GOODWILL (48).

(*e*) Copyrights and trademarks (*Leather Cloth Co v American Leather Cloth Co HL, (1865) 11 HL Cas 523*).

(*f*) Patents.

(g) The benefit of a contract (*Western Abyssinian Mining Syndicate Ltd v CIR KB, (1935) 14 ATC 286*).

(h) Debts (*Measures Bros Ltd v CIR QB, (1900) 82 LT 689*—debts sold as at a date prior to the instrument dutiable even though collected and, therefore, not in existence at the date of the contract).

(j) Cash at bank is a debt due by the bank (*Foley v Hill HL, (1848) 2 HL Cas 28*), see (h); cash in hand may transfer by delivery and will only be dutiable if included in an instrument of conveyance or transfer.

The following, inter alia, have been held not to be property.

(i) A policy of insurance under which no loss has occurred (*Blandy v Herbert KB, (1829) 9 B & C 396*); the principle is doubtful, cf. *Western Abyssinian Mining Syndicate Ltd v CIR*, above.

(ii) Know-how (see *Handley Page v Butterworth HL 1935, 19 TC 328*; cf. *Re Keene CA, [1922] 2 Ch 475*).

(iii) Licence to construct and retain a jetty (*Thames Conservators v CIR QB, (1886) 18 QBD 279*).

Property includes any estate or interest in property and so conveyances or transfers of equitable or limited interests are chargeable.

28.8   CONSIDERATION FOR SALE

In the case of a conveyance or transfer on sale or an agreement or contract for sale, ad valorem duty is calculated on the 'amount or value of the consideration'. A sale normally implies money consideration but the following are also treated as sale considerations for stamp duty purposes:

(a) stock or marketable securities [*SA, s 55*];

(b) debts and other liabilities [*SA, s 57*].

In relation to the transfer or vesting of an estate or interest in land or the grant of a lease or tack where the consideration is property other than cash, stock or debts, ad valorem duty is charged on the market value of the property given as consideration. [*FA 1994, s 241*]. See 25.7 CONSIDERATION.

For further details on the amount on which ad valorem duty is calculated see 25 CONSIDERATION generally.

If the consideration does not comprise money or one of the specified considerations, the transaction will not be treated as a sale for stamp duty purposes unless *FA 1994, s 241* applies.

28.9   SUB-SALES

Where a person has contracted to purchase any property and, before he has obtained a conveyance, contracts to sell that property to a sub-purchaser ad valorem duty is charged only on the consideration for the sub-purchase and not on the two transactions. The property must be conveyed directly to the sub-purchaser for the relief to operate. For the relief to operate the sale consideration moving from the sub-purchaser must be equal to or greater than the value of the property immediately before the contract of sale to him. [*SA, s 58(4)(7); FA 1984, s 112; FA 1985, s 82*]. The relief also applies to cases where the property contracted to be purchased is contracted to be sub-sold in parts to more than one sub-purchaser. The property must be conveyed in parts to the sub-purchasers by the original seller. Ad valorem duty on each conveyance is only charged on the sub-purchase price for that conveyance and the original consideration is ignored. For this relief to apply the aggregate of the sale consideration for the separate parts must be equal to or greater than the value of the whole of the property immediately before the contract for their sale or the first contract for the sale of any of the parts where there are separate contracts. [*SA, s 58(5)(7); FA 1984, s 112; FA 1985, s 82*].

It is understood that the Stamp Office accept that sub-sale relief is available where the original purchase is an exchange of interests in land to which *FA 1994, s 241* applies and the property is conveyed direct to the sub-purchaser. See 25.7 CONSIDERATION.

Relief is also given where the sub-purchaser takes an actual conveyance of the interest of the person immediately selling to him and a later conveyance of the same property from the original seller. If the first conveyance is chargeable with ad valorem duty on the sub-purchase consideration and is duly stamped, the second conveyance will only attract the miscellaneous conveyance or transfer duty of 50p (see 28.12 below) and this will even be reduced to the ad valorem duty paid on the first conveyance, if lower. [*SA, s 58(6)*].

If the sub-purchases do not cover the whole of the property originally contracted to be purchased, duty is payable as follows:

(*a*) on the conveyances to sub-purchasers—duty on those considerations described above;

(*b*) on the conveyance of the remainder of the property to the original purchaser—duty on a proportion of the original purchase price based on the relative values of the part or parts retained and the part or parts sub-sold.

(*Maples v CIR KB, [1914] 3 KB 303*).

For the above reliefs to apply the property sub-sold must be the same as the property originally purchased. See e.g. *Fitch Lovell Ltd v CIR Ch D, [1962] 3 All ER 685* (shares contracted to be sub-sold were different from those originally purchased because of the intervening issue of new shares with prior rights).

28.10 SEVERAL CONVEYANCES

(*a*) **Conveyances of separate parts of property.** Where property is contracted to be sold for one consideration, but the property is conveyed to the purchaser in separate parts, the parties must apportion the whole consideration as they think fit to the separate parts. A distinct consideration must be shown in each conveyance and ad valorem duty is charged on this consideration. [*SA, s 58(1)*].

28.11 Conveyance or Transfer

(b) **Conveyances of separate parts to several persons.** Property may be conveyed in separate parts because, although the purchase contract relates to the whole property for the one consideration, it has been purchased by persons jointly or by a person wholly or partly on behalf of others. In these cases, each instrument of conveyance to the persons by or for whom the property was purchased for distinct parts of the consideration must specify the relevant part of the consideration and ad valorem duty is calculated on that part. [*SA, s 58(2)*].

(c) **Several conveyances to complete title.** Where there are several instruments of conveyance to complete the purchaser's title, ad valorem duty is charged only on the principal instrument. The other instruments bear the 50p miscellaneous conveyance stamp (see 28.12 below), but this is reduced to the amount of the ad valorem duty on the principal instrument, if lower. [*SA, s 58(3)*]. The parties may determine between them which of several instruments is the principal instrument. [*SA, s 61*].

28.11 CONVEYANCE IN CONTEMPLATION OF SALE [*FA 1965, s 90*]

This legislation was introduced to nullify the decision in *William Cory & Son Ltd v CIR HL, [1965] AC 1088*, where a conveyance prior to a sale avoided ad valorem duty as a Conveyance or Transfer on sale.

Any instrument whereby property is conveyed or transferred in contemplation of a sale is treated as a conveyance or transfer on sale for a consideration equal to the **value** of the property.

If the instrument conveys property to which *Sec 90* applies together with other property, *Sec 90* does not affect the amount of duty chargeable in respect of that other property.

ADJUDICATION (2) is required before the instrument is deemed duly stamped.

Provision is made for the repayment of duty paid under *Sec 90* in the following cases.

(a) Where the contemplated sale did not take place and the property has been reconveyed or retransferred to the person who conveyed or transferred it (or a person to whom his rights have been transmitted on death or bankruptcy), the duty repaid is the amount paid less any duty which would have been payable on the first conveyance (e.g. miscellaneous conveyance duty of 50p—see 28.12 below).

(b) Where the sale has taken place for a consideration which is less than the value on which duty was paid, the amount repaid is the difference between the duty paid and ad valorem duty on the actual consideration.

In each case the claim must be made within two years of the execution of the instrument of conveyance or transfer charged under *Sec 90*.

28.12 MISCELLANEOUS CONVEYANCE OR TRANSFER

The fixed duty of 50p applies to conveyances or transfers which are not either sales of property or otherwise caught under *FA 1994, ss 241* and *242* (see 25.7 and 25.9 CONSIDERATION). [*SA, 1 Sch*].

It is provided that every instrument and decree or order of a court or commissioners whereby any property, on an occasion other than a sale or mortgage, is transferred or vested in any person is charged with duty as a conveyance or transfer of property. [*SA, s 62*].

Examples of instruments which attract the 50p fixed duty are

(*a*) conveyances or transfers where no beneficial interest passes;

(*b*) conveyances or transfers by way of security;

(*c*) conveyances or transfers for a consideration not taken into account for ad valorem duty (see 28.8 above);

(*d*) distribution of assets by a liquidator to shareholders in satisfaction of their rights in a winding-up (*Henty and Constable (Brewers) Ltd v CIR CA, [1961] 3 All ER 1146*).

However, where permitted, instruments certified in accordance with the *Stamp Duty (Exempt Instruments) Regulations 1987 (SI 1987 No 516)* are exempted from the fixed 50p duty and do not have to be presented to the Commissioners either for duty or ADJUDICATION (2). Thus, for example, the inclusion of the appropriate certificate in an instrument within (*d*) above will exempt the instrument from the 50p duty and the need to present it to the Commissioners for duty or adjudication. See 39 EXEMPT INSTRUMENTS. Not all instruments liable to the fixed 50p duty can be so certified under these regulations. Examples of instruments which cannot be certified are

(i) conveyances or transfers from a beneficial owner to his nominee and vice versa;

(ii) conveyances or transfers from one nominee to another nominee for the same beneficial owner; and

(iii) conveyances or transfers by way of security.

29   Court Orders

29.1   A decree or order of a court or commissioners whereby property (or any estate or interest in property) on the sale thereof is transferred to or vested in a purchaser is treated as a conveyance on sale liable to ad valorem duty as a CONVEYANCE OR TRANSFER (28) on sale. [*SA, s 54*]. This includes foreclosure decrees. [*FA 1898, s 6*]. See 45 FORECLOSURE.

29.2   A decree or order which vests or transfers property otherwise than by sale or mortgage is chargeable with the fixed 50p duty applicable to a miscellaneous CONVEYANCE OR TRANSFER (28). [*SA, s 62*]. This includes vesting orders.

29.3   Court Orders

29.3   The date of execution of an order is the date when it is drawn and dated (*Sun Alliance Insurance Ltd v CIR Ch D 1971, [1972] Ch 133*).

29.4   ADJUDICATION (2) is required in practice for orders made under the *Variation of Trusts Act 1958* and *Companies Act 1985, s 427* (reconstruction or amalgamation of companies) and the solicitors involved are required to give an appropriate undertaking to the court.

30   Covenants

30.1   For the treatment of covenants relating to annuities and other periodic sums, see 16 BONDS and 7 ANNUITIES. Covenants on the creation and sale of annuities are dealt with as conveyances on sale.

30.2   The former head of charge 'Covenant' which charged duty at 50p or the amount of the ad valorem duty on the consideration if less, was repealed by *FA 1985, s 85, 24 Sch (d)*.

31   Declaration of Trust

31.1   Declarations of trust in writing concerning any property are liable to a fixed duty of 50p. This charge does not apply to trusts created by wills. [*SA, 1 Sch*].

31.2   The charge only applies to written declarations and does not affect oral declarations concerning personalty. A declaration of trust may attract ad valorem duty as a CONVEYANCE OR TRANSFER (28) on sale. See 28.5(*d*).

See generally 75 TRUSTS AND TRUSTEES.

32 Deeds

32.1 The fixed duty of 50p charged on miscellaneous deeds, being deeds of any kind not otherwise described in *SA, 1 Sch* was abolished by *FA 1985, s 85, 24 Sch (e)*.

33 Denoting Stamp

33.1 DUTY PAID DENOTING STAMP

A denoting stamp is used where the duty with which an instrument is chargeable depends upon the duty paid on another document. The payment of duty on that other document is denoted on the instrument by the Commissioners. [*SA, s 11*].

33.2 A denoting stamp is required in the following cases.

(*a*) A DUPLICATE OR COUNTERPART (35) of an instrument liable to higher duty than 50p attracts 50p if it bears a denoting stamp 'Duplicate or Counterpart—original fully and properly stamped'. A denoting stamp is not required for a counterpart of a lease if the counterpart is not executed by the lessor or grantor. [*SA, s 72*].

(*b*) A CONVEYANCE OR TRANSFER (28) to a purchaser or sub-purchaser under a contract or agreement which has attracted ad valorem duty is not liable to ad valorem duty if the earlier payment of duty is denoted by a 'duty paid, ad valorem' stamp. [*SA, s 59*]. See 6.9, 6.12 AGREEMENT FOR SALE.

(*c*) A conveyance, transfer, lease or tack requires a 'duty paid, ad valorem' stamp where the conveyance or transfer of an interest in land is subject to an agreement for a lease or tack for a term exceeding 35 years or where a lease or tack is granted for a lease for a term exceeding 35 years. The duty paid on the AGREEMENT FOR LEASE (5) is denoted on the conveyance, transfer, lease or tack. [*FA 1984, s 111(2)(3)*].

(*d*) A lease or tack which does not contain a certificate that there is no agreement to which it gives effect. To be duly stamped such a lease or tack must be stamped with a stamp denoting either that there is an agreement to which it gives effect which is not chargeable with duty or the duty paid on the agreement.

(*e*) An inland or overseas bearer instrument chargeable on transfer given in substitution for a like instrument duly stamped ad valorem is charged with duty of 10p if it is denoted by a stamp 'original duly stamped'. [*FA 1963, s 60(8)*]. See 13 BEARER INSTRUMENTS.

33.3 Denoting Stamp

33.3 The Commissioners usually require production of the original stamped instrument (duty on which is to be denoted on the later instrument) but will accept copies issued by the Land Registry of documents registered there if the duty is clearly shown.

33.4 A denoting stamp does not indicate that the original document has been duly stamped; this is only possible if the original instrument has been adjudicated. See 2 ADJUDICATION.

33.5 OTHER DENOTING STAMPS

In the following cases denoting stamps are required but do not indicate duty being paid on any other instrument.

(*a*) A bearer instrument chargeable on issue must be produced to the Commissioners before issue and stamped with a denoting stamp. This stamp precedes the payment of duty (which is within six weeks of issue) but the instrument is deemed to be duly stamped. [*FA 1963, s 60(3)*]. See 13.5(*a*) BEARER INSTRUMENTS.

(*b*) The transfer of stock on sale to a market-maker does not attract any duty if it bears a stamp denoting that it is not chargeable with any duty. [*FA 1986, s 81(1)(2)*]. See 72.9 SHARES AND SECURITIES.

---

34 Depositary Receipts

Note. The stamp duty and stamp duty reserve tax charges in relation to depository receipts were to be abolished from a date to be appointed by statutory instrument. [*FA 1990, ss 108–111*]. But see 1.1 INTRODUCTION.

34.1 A depositary receipt scheme involves the issue by a bank of depositary receipts which are backed by shares held by the bank's nominee. The depositary receipts can be in registered or bearer form and will acknowledge the right of the holder of the receipt to the underlying shares and to any dividends and rights issues. In practice the depositary receipts will be bought and sold in overseas stock markets without attracting ad valorem stamp duty. The bank's nominee will remain the registered holder of the underlying shares or securities in the share register of the company whose shares have been 'converted' into depositary receipts. The increasing use of depositary receipts, particularly American Depositary Receipts or 'ADRs' representing shares in UK companies, led to an erosion of the yield of ad valorem stamp duty from share purchases. A special 'entry' charge of three times the normal rate of ad valorem duty on a CONVEYANCE OR TRANSFER (28) on sale was therefore imposed by *FA 1986* on the issue, transfer or appropriation of shares and securities in connection with the issue of depositary receipts. The special 'entry' charge of three times the normal duty is designed to compensate for the fact that the depositary receipts will be traded subsequently free of ad valorem duty.

The special charge can be either stamp duty (see 34.2 below) or STAMP DUTY RESERVE TAX (73) (see 34.3 below) depending on the circumstances.

34.2 STAMP DUTY

Stamp duty at the special rate is charged on an instrument which *transfers* 'relevant securities' of a UK incorporated company to a person

(*a*) whose business consists exclusively of holding 'relevant securities' as nominee or agent for a person whose business is or includes issuing depositary receipts for 'relevant securities'; or

(*b*) who is specified by a statutory instrument and whose business is or includes issuing depositary receipts for 'relevant securities'; or

(*c*) who is specified by a statutory instrument and whose business does not consist exclusively of holding 'relevant securities' as nominee or agent for an issuer of depositary receipts.

In relation to 'relevant securities' consisting of units representing paired shares of the type issued by Eurotunnel, the foreign company is treated as a company incorporated in the UK.

[*FA 1986, s 67(1)(6)–(8); FA 1988, s 143(6)*].

'Relevant securities' are shares or stock or marketable securities of any company wherever incorporated. [*FA 1986, s 69(3)*].

A 'depositary receipt for relevant securities' is an instrument acknowledging that a person holds relevant securities or evidence of the right to receive them and that another person is entitled to rights, whether expressed as units or otherwise, in or in relation to relevant securities of the same kind, including the right to receive such securities (or evidence of the right to receive them) from the first person. [*FA 1986, s 69(1)*].

Where the instrument of transfer attracts duty under the CONVEYANCE OR TRANSFER (28) on sale head duty is charged at the special rate of £1.50 per £100 or part of £100 of the amount or value of the sale consideration. Where the instrument instead attracts duty under the 'conveyance or transfer of any kind not hereinbefore described' head, duty is charged at the special rate also instead of the fixed 50p duty which this head of charge normally imposes. [*FA 1986, s 67(2)(3)*]. A transfer of 'relevant securities' of a UK incorporated company between corporate nominees resident in the UK attracts only a maximum 50p duty. [*FA 1986, s 67(9)*].

Where the instrument attracts duty under the 'conveyance or transfer of any kind not hereinbefore described' head the special rate is reduced to £1.00 per £100 or part of £100 of the value of the securities where the transferor is a 'qualified dealer' in securities of the kind concerned or his nominee but is not a 'market maker' in those securities and the transfer is in the course of the dealer's business. The instrument must contain a statement to this effect. [*FA 1986, s 67(4)*].

A person is a 'qualified dealer' if he is a member of a recognised stock exchange or is designated a qualified dealer by the Treasury. [*FA 1986, s 69(6)*].

A person is a 'market maker' if he holds himself out at all normal times under The International Stock Exchange rules as willing to buy and sell securities of the kind concerned at a price specified by him and is recognised as doing so by the Council of The International Stock Exchange. [*FA 1986, s 69(7)*].

An issuer of depositary receipts for 'relevant securities' of UK incorporated companies and a person whose business includes (but is not exclusively) holding such securities as nominee or agent for an issuer is required to notify the Commissioners of that fact within one month of the issuing of the receipts or holding the relevant securities. A fine of up to £1,000 is imposed for failing to do so. [*FA 1986, s 68(1)(2)(4)*]. A UK incorporated company which becomes aware that its shares are held by an issuer of depositary receipts or his nominee or agent is also required to notify the Commissioners of that fact within one month of becoming so aware. A fine of up to £100 can be imposed for failing to do so. [*FA 1986, s 68(3)(5)*].

34.3 STAMP DUTY RESERVE TAX

STAMP DUTY RESERVE TAX (73) at the special rate is charged where 'chargeable securities' are *issued, transferred* to or *appropriated* by a person who holds such securities as nominee or agent for an issuer of depositary receipts as part of an arrangement for the issuer to issue depositary receipts. [*FA 1986, s 93(1)*].

For the definition of 'chargeable securities' see 73 STAMP DUTY RESERVE TAX.

In relation to the *transfer* of 'chargeable securities' any ad valorem stamp duty chargeable on the instrument of transfer (see 34.2 above) cancels the equivalent amount of the reserve tax chargeable up to the full amount of the reserve tax. [*FA 1986, s 93(7)*].

The special rate is £1.50 for every £100 or part of £100

(*a*) of the issue price, where securities are *issued*;

(*b*) of the amount or value of the consideration where the securities are *transferred*; or

(*c*) of the *value* of the securities, in any other case.

[*FA 1986, s 93(4)*].

In relation to the *transfer* of securities where the instrument of transfer attracts stamp duty under the 'conveyance or transfer of any kind not hereinbefore described' head the special rate is reduced to £1.00 per £100 or part of £100 where the transfer is to a 'qualified dealer' in securities of the kind concerned or his nominee but is not a 'market maker' in the securities concerned and the transfer is in the course of the dealer's business. The instrument must contain a statement to this effect. [*FA 1986, s 93(5)*].

A person is a 'qualified dealer' if he is a member of a recognised stock exchange or is designated a qualified dealer by the Treasury. [*FA 1986, s 94(5)*].

A person is a 'market maker' if he holds himself out at all normal times under The International Stock Exchange rules as willing to buy and sell securities of the kind concerned at a price specified by him and is recognised as doing so by the Council of The International Stock Exchange. [*FA 1986, s 94(6)*].

The person liable to pay the reserve tax is the issuer of the depositary receipts except where securities are *transferred* and the issuer is not resident in the UK and has no UK branch or agency in which case the transferee is liable for the tax. [*FA 1986, s 93(8)(9)*].

There is no charge to tax under *Sec 93* in the following circumstances:

(*a*) a transfer of securities between corporate nominees who are resident in the UK and whose businesses are exclusively that of holding 'relevant securities' as nominees for an issuer of depositary receipts;

(*b*) the *issue, transfer*, or *appropriation* of an inland bearer instrument which is not a renounceable letter of allotment with a life of six months or less, (see 13 BEARER INSTRUMENTS);

(*c*) the *issue* by one company of securities in exchange for shares in another company where the first company has control of the second (or will have control as a result of the share for share exchange).

[*FA 1986, s 95*].

---

35   Duplicate or Counterpart

35.1 Duplicates or counterparts of any instrument chargeable to duty bear duty of 50p or the same duty as the original instrument if lower. [*SA, 1 Sch; FA 1974, s 49, 11 Sch Part II*].

35.2 A duplicate or counterpart (other than the counterpart of a lease not executed by or on behalf of the lessor or grantor) is not deemed duly stamped unless it is stamped as an original instrument or bears a stamp denoting that the correct duty has been paid on the original document. [*SA, s 72*]. See 33.2 DENOTING STAMP.

36   Evidence

36.1   An unstamped or insufficiently-stamped document will not be admitted as evidence in any civil proceedings, even for a collateral purpose (*Fengl v Fengl PDA, [1914] P 274*), nor will secondary evidence thereof (*Rippiner v Wright KB, (1819) 2 B & Ald 478*). Where the wrong stamp has been used, the instrument is not duly stamped and will not be admitted in evidence (*Ashling v Boon Ch D, [1891] 1 Ch 568* where an adhesive postage stamp appropriate to a receipt had been used on an instrument which should have been stamped with an appropriated 'bill or note' stamp). However, if the instrument may be stamped after execution (see 63.1 PAYMENT OF DUTY OR TAX), it may be received in evidence on payment to the Court of the duty and any penalty plus £1. [*SA, s 14(1)*].

36.2   Notwithstanding the statutory provisions, it has been the practice of the Court to allow an unstamped document to be used on the personal under-taking by the solicitors to stamp it (see e.g. *Re Coolgardie Goldfields Ltd Ch D, [1900] 1 Ch 475*) though doubt has been cast on this practice where deliberate disregard of the stamp duty legislation is involved (*Lloyds and Scottish Finance Ltd v Prentice CA 1977, 121 Sol Jo 847*). The General Council of the Bar regards a stamp duty objection as unprofessional except in a revenue case or where the stamping defect goes to the root of the validity of the document.

36.3   An unstamped or insufficiently-stamped document is admissible in evidence in criminal cases. (See *Saunders v Edwards CA, [1987] 2 All ER 651*.)

37   Exchange or Partition

37.1   For instruments executed after 7 December 1993 stamp duty under the head 'Exchange or Excambion' and *SA, s 73* have ceased to apply to the exchange of freehold property. Instead, *FA 1994, s 241* now treats exchanges of freehold property and other interests in land as liable to ad valorem duty under the head CONVEYANCE OR TRANSFER (28) on sale. For an explanation of this change and how in practice the Inland Revenue will permit a double charge of duty to be avoided see 25.7 and 25.8 CONSIDERATION.

37.2   For the position regarding instruments executed before 8 December 1993 see the third edition of this work.

37.3 In the case of a partition or division of any estate or interest in land where consideration exceeding £100 is paid or given, ad valorem duty is charged on the consideration at the rate applicable to a CONVEYANCE OR TRANSFER (28) on sale. The nil rate of duty is available if a CERTIFICATE OF VALUE (19) is given in respect of the consideration. Where a sum in respect of value added tax is paid on a partition the Stamp Office treat this payment as equality money.

37.4 In any other case a partition is charged with a fixed duty of 50p under the head 'Partition' in *SA, 1 Sch*. Although a partition is not a sale (*Henniker v Henniker QB 1852, 1 E & B 54*) it is important that following *FA 1994, s 241*, a partition of land is not drafted as an exchange of beneficial interests in jointly owned property because this may be treated by the Stamp Office as series of sales and liable to ad valorem duty on each leg. (See 25.7 and 25.8 CONSIDERATION).

37.5 The partition of any property other than an estate or interest in land is liable to a fixed duty of 50p even if there is equality money.

38 Execution

38.1 In the case of instruments not under seal, execution means signing. [*SA, s 122(1)*]. However, if execution is conditional, as with a document executed and delivered in escrow, the execution is not operative until the condition has been fulfilled (*Terrapin International Ltd v CIR Ch D, [1976] 2 All ER 461; Crane Fruehauf Ltd v CIR Ch D, [1974] 1 All ER 811*). This has been confirmed by *SA, s 122(1A)* which treats a deed as executed when it is delivered, or if delivered subject to conditions, when the conditions are fulfilled. [*FA 1994, s 239*]. The Stamp Office normally accepts as the date of execution of an instrument the date appearing on its face; and see 29.3 COURT ORDERS.

The date of execution is relevant, inter alia, to the time of payment of duty (see 63.1 PAYMENT OF DUTY OR TAX); for the importance of place of execution see 20 CHARGEABILITY.

39 Exempt Instruments

39.1 Numerous heads of charge in *SA* have been abolished by subsequent Finance Acts. In addition to outright repeals of heads of charge there are exemptions contained within existing heads of charge e.g. the exemptions under the 'bearer instrument' head. There are also some general exemptions from all stamp duties e.g. the instruments mentioned at the end of *SA, 1 Sch*. There are also the various exemptions and reliefs such as those relating to ASSOCIATED COMPANIES (12), COMPANY REORGANISATIONS (23) and LOAN CAPITAL AND DEBENTURES (55) for example. There is also a general exemption for conveyances, transfers or leases to a Minister of the Crown or to the Treasury Solicitor. [*FA 1987, s 55*].

39.2 EXEMPT INSTRUMENTS REGULATIONS

[*The Stamp Duty (Exempt Instruments) Regulations 1987 (SI 1987 No 516)*]

In addition to the above exemptions, the Treasury have made regulations under *FA 1985, s 87* which apply to certain instruments executed on or after 1 May 1987 which would normally attract a fixed 50p duty under the heads of charge 'CONVEYANCE OR TRANSFER (28.12) of any kind not hereinbefore described' or 'Dispositions in Scotland of any property or of any right or interest therein not described in this Schedule'. Instruments which have been correctly certified under the regulations are exempt from these particular 50p duties and do not have to be presented to the Commissioners either for payment of duty or for ADJUDICATION (2). They can be sent direct to registrars for recording and registration. Although a registrar is always entitled to require an ADJUDICATION (2) it is understood that the Land Registry for example will accept a certified instrument for registration without requiring ADJUDICATION (2) so long as it appears to fall within one of the categories specified in the schedule to the regulations and the certificate has been given properly (see 39.3 below).

Not all instruments attracting these fixed 50p duties can be dealt with by certification. Only the instruments of a kind specified in the schedule to the regulations are exempt and those are instruments effecting any one or more of the following transactions only.

(*a*) The vesting of property subject to a trust in the trustees of the trust on the appointment of a new trustee, or in the continuing trustees on the retirement of a trustee.

(*b*) The conveyance or transfer of property the subject of a specific devise or legacy to the beneficiary named in the will (or his nominee).

(*c*) The conveyance or transfer of property which forms part of an intestate's estate to the person entitled on intestacy (or his nominee).

(*d*) The appropriation of property within *Sec 84(4)* of the *Finance Act 1985* (death: appropriation in satisfaction of a general legacy of money) or

Sec 84(5) or *(7)* of that Act (death: appropriation in satisfaction of any interest of surviving spouse and in Scotland also of any interest of issue).

(*e*) The conveyance or transfer of property which forms part of the residuary estate of a testator to a beneficiary (or his nominee) entitled solely by virtue of his entitlement under the will.

(*f*) The conveyance or transfer of property out of a settlement in or towards satisfaction of a beneficiary's interest, not being an interest acquired for money or money's worth, being a conveyance or transfer constituting a distribution of property in accordance with the provisions of the settlement.

(*g*) The conveyance or transfer of property on and in consideration only of marriage to a party to the marriage (or his nominee) or to trustees to be held on the terms of a settlement made in consideration only of the marriage.

(*h*) The conveyance or transfer of property within *Sec 83(1)* of the *Finance Act 1985* (transfers in connection with divorce etc.).

(*i*) The conveyance or transfer by the liquidator of property which formed part of the assets of the company in liquidation to a shareholder of that company (or his nominee) in or towards satisfaction of the shareholder's rights on a winding-up.

(*j*) The grant in fee simple of an easement in or over land for no consideration in money or money's worth.

(*k*) The grant of a servitude for no consideration in money or money's worth.

(*l*) The conveyance or transfer of property operating as a voluntary disposition inter vivos for no consideration in money or money's worth nor any consideration referred to in *Sec 57* of the *Stamp Act 1891* (conveyance in consideration of a debt etc.).

(*m*) The conveyance or transfer of property by an instrument within *Sec 84(1)* of the *Finance Act 1985* (death: varying disposition).

39.3 The form of wording of the certificate suggested by the Commissioners is: 'I/We hereby certify that this instrument falls within category . . . in the *Schedule* to the *Stamp Duty (Exempt Instruments) Regulations 1987*'.

This certificate should be included in, endorsed on or attached to the instrument. Where the certificate is endorsed after the instrument is executed the certificate must also contain a description of the instrument, e.g. title, date, parties and property passing. In the case of a CONVEYANCE OR TRANSFER (28) of land the Commissioners prefer the certificate to be included in or endorsed on the instrument and not attached to it. Endorsement on the reverse of a share transfer is acceptable to the Commissioners. The certificate should be signed by the transferor or grantor or his solicitor or duly authorised agent such as a licensed conveyancer, accountant etc.

39.4   Exempt Instruments

Where the certificate is not signed by the transferor, grantor or his solicitor it should contain a statement of the capacity in which the signatory signs, that he is authorised to sign and that he gives the certificate from his own knowledge of the facts stated in it.

39.4 Various instruments which transfer property otherwise than on sale and which attract the fixed 50p duty are not covered by the regulations and remain liable to duty. Examples are

(*a*) transfers from a beneficial owner to his nominee and vice versa and transfers between nominees for the same beneficial owner;

(*b*) transfers by way of security for a loan or retransfer on repayment of the loan; and

(*c*) transfers from the trustees of a Profit Sharing Scheme to a participant.

---

40   Extra-Statutory Concessions

[Extra-Statutory Concessions—Revenue booklet IR 1 (1994)].

40.1 STAMP ALLOWANCE ON LOST DOCUMENTS

Allowance of the stamp duty on lost documents is made either by repayment, where replicas have been stamped or by free stamping of the replicas.

40.2 STAMPING OF REPLICAS OF DOCUMENTS WHICH HAVE BEEN SPOILT OR LOST

Where the stamp duty is allowed on a document because it has been spoilt or lost and replaced by a replica but the duty has been increased so that the amount to be impressed on the replica is more than the amount allowable on the original, the additional duty is impressed free of charge.

40.3 TRANSFER OF STOCK FROM PERSONS TO THEMSELVES OPERATING AS AN EXECUTORS' ASSENT

Stamp duty is not claimed on a transfer of stock in a company registered in England, Wales or Northern Ireland from a person to himself (or from two or more persons to themselves) which operates as an executors' assent. The point does not arise in relation to companies registered in Scotland. See 11 ASSENTS.

40.4 **TRANSFER OF ASSETS BETWEEN NON-PROFIT MAKING BODIES WITH SIMILAR OBJECTS**

When the reconstruction of a non-profit making body with objects in a field of public interest such as education, community work or scientific research, or the amalgamation of two or more such bodies involves a transfer to the successor body of assets for which there passes no consideration in money or money's worth, the instruments of transfer are treated as exempt from ad valorem stamp duty and charged 50p fixed duty only. There must be sufficient identity between the members of the transferor and transferee bodies. The rules of both must prohibit the distribution of assets to members and provide that on a winding-up the assets can only be transferred to a similar body subject to like restrictions.

---

41   Failure to Stamp

41.1 In general, stamp duties, which are chargeable on instruments, are not recoverable by the Commissioners by direct recovery procedures. Exemptions to this rule are dealt with at 63.3 PAYMENT OF DUTY OR TAX.

41.2 Enforcement of the duties is achieved by providing that an instrument is not to be given in EVIDENCE (36) or to be available for any purpose whatever unless it is duly stamped in accordance with the law in force at the time when it was executed. [*SA, s 14(4)*]. In addition, the enrolment or registration of an instrument not duly stamped gives rise to a fine of £10. [*SA, s 17*]. Conditions precluding stamp duty objections or agreements for undertaking liability in the event of absence or insufficiency of stamp are void. [*SA, s 117*].

41.3 INSTRUMENTS (49) may generally be stamped late on payment of general penalties and interest (see 63.1 PAYMENT OF DUTY OR TAX) and specific PENALTIES AND OFFENCES (64) may arise.

41.4 In relation to agreements for the sale of shares or securities STAMP DUTY RESERVE TAX (73) can arise unless an instrument transferring the shares or securities to the purchaser or his nominee is executed and duly stamped within two months of the agreement.

42 Family Arrangements and Divorce

42.1 FAMILY ARRANGEMENTS

Ad valorem duty under the head CONVEYANCE OR TRANSFER (28) on sale is not chargeable on an instrument which varies a disposition of property effected by a will or under the law of intestacy or otherwise within two years after a person's death. The instrument can be executed by all or any of the persons who benefit or would benefit under the dispositions. The exemption does not apply where the variation is made for any consideration in money or money's worth other than consideration consisting of the variation of another of the dispositions. The exemption applies whether or not the administration of the estate is complete or the property distributed according to the original dispositions. [*FA 1985, s 84(1)–(3)*].

42.2 Where property is appropriated by a personal representative in or towards satisfaction of a general legacy of money, no ad valorem duty is chargeable. Also ad valorem duty is not charged in an intestacy on the appropriation of property by a personal representative for clearing any interest of the surviving spouse in the intestate's estate. This includes the capital value of a life interest elected to be redeemed under the *Intestates Estate Act 1952*. [*FA 1985, s 84(4)–(6)*]. See 11 ASSENTS.

42.3 In order for the instrument to be exempt from ad valorem duty it used to be necessary to have it adjudicated and stamped with a fixed 50p duty. [*FA 1985, s 84(8)(9)*]. Now, under the *Stamp Duty (Exempt Instruments) Regulations 1987 (SI 1987 No 516)* such instruments do not have to be produced to the Stamp Office for stamping or ADJUDICATION (2) provided they are properly certified in accordance with the regulations. See 39 EXEMPT INSTRUMENTS.

42.4 DIVORCE

Ad valorem duty under the head CONVEYANCE OR TRANSFER (28) on sale is not chargeable on an instrument by which property is conveyed or transferred from one party to a marriage to the other. This is provided that the instrument is executed for one or more of the following reasons.

(*a*) A court order made on granting a divorce, annulment of marriage or judicial separation.

(*b*) A court order made in connection with the dissolution or annulment of a marriage or a judicial separation and the court order is made at any time after the dissolution, annulment or separation.

(*c*) An agreement made between the parties in contemplation of or otherwise in connection with the dissolution or annulment of their marriage or judicial separation.

[*FA 1985, s 83(1)*].

74

42.5 No stamping or adjudication is required provided the instrument is properly certified. See 39 EXEMPT INSTRUMENTS.

43   Fixed Duties

43.1 Fixed duties are those charged without regard to the value of the transaction. For duties calculated by reference to value, see 4 AD VALOREM DUTIES. Many obsolete fixed duties were abolished by *FA 1985, s 85, 24 Sch*, including the 50p duties on the appointment of a new trustee, deeds of covenant, deeds and powers of attorney.

43.2 The fixed duty now most commonly met is the miscellaneous CONVEYANCE OR TRANSFER (28) duty of 50p. The practical importance of this duty has been greatly diminished by the *Stamp Duty (Exempt Instruments) Regulations 1987, (SI 1987 No 516)*. See 39 EXEMPT INSTRUMENTS.

43.3 Other fixed duties dealt with in this book are:

Heading	Duty
CLEARANCE SERVICES (22)	50p
DECLARATION OF TRUST (31)	50p
DEPOSITARY RECEIPTS (34)	50p
DUPLICATE OR COUNTERPART (35)	50p
EXCHANGE OR PARTITION (37)	50p
FAMILY ARRANGEMENTS AND DIVORCE (42)	50p
LEASES (53)—small furnished lettings	£1
—miscellaneous	£2
RELEASE AND RENUNCIATION (69)	50p
SURRENDERS (74)	50p

44   Flotations, etc.

44.1 The abolition of CAPITAL DUTY (18) by *FA 1988, s 141* removed not only a potential charge to capital duty on the raising of share capital but also the need to structure the arrangements in particular ways in order to attract exemption from capital duty where available. For example, it was often necessary to avoid the use of renounceable letters of allotment and to ensure that the consideration shares allotted were actually issued and registered in the names of the vendors (see *Tillotson v CIR CA, [1933] 1 KB 134*). It is still necessary to consider the impact of STAMP DUTY RESERVE TAX (73) in connection with agreements to transfer renounceable letters of allotment and acceptance. Such agreements are a feature of flotations etc. and careful attention must be paid to each step in a particular transaction in order to ascertain whether a tax charge can arise and if so whether it is possible to alter the arrangements to avoid the charge. What follows examines some of the types of transactions commonly met.

44.2   **OFFERS FOR SALE**

An offer for sale of new shares for cash involves the issue by the company raising share capital of a nil paid renounceable letter of allotment to the issuing house. The nil paid renounceable letter of allotment will be deemed to become fully paid as soon as the admission of the company's shares to the Official List of the Stock Exchange comes into effect. The issuing house issues fully paid renounceable letters of acceptance to the applicants and dealings in these letters then occur. Once the renunciation period has ended the issuing house renounces its letter of allotment in favour of the ultimate holders of the renounceable letters of acceptance who will become the registered shareholders. Stamp duty reserve tax is charged on each sale of the renounceable letters of acceptance during the renunciation period. Stamp duty reserve tax is not charged on the issue of the renounceable letters of acceptance by the issuing house provided the conditions of *FA 1986, s 89A(2)* are met (see 44.8 below). No other stamp duty or stamp duty reserve tax charges should arise.

44.3   An offer for sale by the existing shareholders may involve the allotment of bonus shares to the existing shareholders represented by fully paid renounceable letters of allotment. The issuing house will purchase the renounceable letters of allotment and issue renounceable letters of acceptance to the applicants and dealings in these letters may then occur. Once the renunciation period has ended the ultimate holders of the renounceable letters of acceptance will become the registered shareholders. Stamp duty reserve tax is not charged on the purchase by the issuing house of the renounceable letters of allotment provided the conditions of *FA 1986, s 89A(1)* are met (see 44.8 below). Nor is stamp duty reserve tax charged on the issue of the renounceable letters of acceptance provided the conditions of *FA 1986, s 89A(2)* are met. The tax is charged on each sale of the renounceable letters of acceptance during the renunciation period. No other stamp duty or stamp duty reserve tax charges should arise.

44.4   An offer for sale by the existing shareholders may involve the sale of their existing shares in addition to or instead of the sale of newly allotted bonus shares (see 45.3 above). The issuing house agrees to purchase the existing shares from the shareholders who grant powers of attorney to enable the issuing house to transfer the shares to whoever the issuing house nominates.

The issuing house issues renounceable letters of acceptance to the applicants and dealings in those letters may then occur. Once the renunciation period has ended the ultimate holders of the renounceable letters of acceptance will become the new registered shareholders. Stamp duty reserve tax is not charged on the purchase of the shares by the issuing house provided the conditions of *FA 1986, s 89A(1)* are met (see 45.8 below). Nor is there a stamp duty reserve tax charge on the issue of the renounceable letters of acceptance by the issuing house so long as the conditions of *FA 1986, s 89A(3)* are met (see 45.8 below). The tax is charged on each sale of the renounceable letters of allotment during the renunciation period. Stamp duty will be charged on the transfer of the shares themselves from the existing shareholders to the original applicants or where the letters of acceptance have been renounced, to the ultimate renouncees of the letters of acceptance. Where a renounceable letter of acceptance has been retained by the applicant for the shares, and in due course the shares are transferred to him, there will have been no stamp duty reserve tax charge and the only charge will be a stamp duty charge on the share transfer calculated according to the average market price of the shares during the renunciation period. However, where the renounceable letters of acceptance have been sold stamp duty reserve tax will have been charged on each sale including the sale to the ultimate renouncee, but stamp duty will also be charged on the transfer of the shares themselves to the ultimate renouncee. This problem is sometimes referred to as 'the double hit' and occurs because *FA 1986, s 88(2)(3)* does not permit the stamp duty on the share transfer to cancel the stamp duty reserve tax charge on the sale of the letter of acceptance to the ultimate renouncee (see 73 STAMP DUTY RESERVE TAX). In particular cases the vendor may agree to bear the stamp duty charge and this will be stated in the relevant prospectus.

44.5 RIGHTS ISSUES

A rights issue will involve the issue by the company concerned of fully paid renounceable letters of allotment or nil paid provisional renounceable letters of allotment to the existing shareholders. Once the renunciation period has ended the ultimate holders of the renounceable letters of allotment will become the registered holders of the new shares. Stamp duty reserve tax is charged on each sale of the renounceable letters of allotment during the renunciation period according to the price paid by each renouncee. No stamp duty reserve tax or stamp duty is charged on the issue of the renounceable letters of allotment or on the issue of the shares themselves at the end of the renunciation period.

44.6 VENDOR PLACINGS

A vendor placing occurs when an acquiring company acquires the shares (or undertaking) of an unlisted company from the vendors in consideration of the allotment to the vendors of shares in the acquiring company. The vendors will then sell these shares in the market with the assistance of an issuing house. Following the abolition of capital duty there is normally no need to issue consideration shares to the vendors which was a necessary condition for obtaining capital duty exemption; it is sufficient to allot the consideration shares on renounceable letters of allotment. No stamp duty arises on the issue of the renounceable letters of allotment to the vendors. Stamp duty reserve tax may not be charged on the purchase of the renounceable letters of allotment by the issuing house for sale to the placees provided the conditions of *FA 1986, s 89A(1)* are met. In particular it appears that the Revenue have not yet reached a firm view on whether a vendor placing can be regarded as an 'offer to the public' (see 44.8 below). Stamp duty reserve tax is charged on any sale of the renounceable letters of allotment during the renunciation period. No stamp duty or stamp duty reserve tax charges arise on the registration of the holders as members of the company at the end of the renunciation period. Stamp duty will normally be charged on the transfer of the shares or assets of the target company to the acquiring company.

44.7 UNDERWRITING

The underwriting of shares can give rise to stamp duty and stamp duty reserve tax charges. See 76 UNDERWRITING.

44.8 EXCEPTIONS FOR PUBLIC ISSUES

An unintended effect of the introduction of stamp duty reserve tax was to impose additional tax charges in connection with flotations and new issues where an issuing house, acting traditionally as principal, bought and sold shares or renounceable letters of allotment or acceptance as part of the arrangements. This quickly led to issuing houses acting as 'agents to procure' purchasers and subscribers rather than as principals in order to avoid the stamp duty reserve tax charges that would apply if they acted as principals. The Inland Revenue treat only the principals and not their agents in a transaction as being A or B for the purpose of *FA 1986, s 87*. However, when an issuing house acts as agent rather than as principal, members of the public are not offered a common root of title i.e. the issuing house, and instead face the risk of the vendors having a bad title or going bankrupt or dying. In an attempt to solve the problem *FA 1986, s 89A* (inserted by *F(No 2)A 1987, s 100*) provides that stamp duty reserve tax shall not apply where the issuing house acts as principal as regards the following.

(*a*) An agreement to transfer securities other than units under a unit trust scheme to B or B's nominee if

    (i) the agreement is part of an arrangement entered into by B in the ordinary course of B's business as an issuing house under which B is to offer the securities for sale to the public,

    (ii) the agreement is conditional upon the admission of the securities to the Official List of the Stock Exchange,

    (iii) the consideration under the agreement for each security is the same as the price at which B is to offer the security for sale, and

    (iv) B sells the securities in accordance with the arrangement referred to in (i) above.

This is intended to except from stamp duty reserve tax the purchase by the issuing house of existing registered shares or fully paid renounceable letters of allotment representing bonus shares held by existing shareholders as part of an offer for sale (see 44.3 and 44.4 above).

(*b*) An agreement if the securities to which the agreement relates are newly subscribed securities other than units in a unit trust scheme and

    (i) the agreement is made in pursuance of an offer to the public made by A under an arrangement entered into in the ordinary course of A's business as an issuing house,

    (ii) a right of allotment in respect of, or to subscribe for, the securities has been acquired by A under an agreement which is part of the arrangement,

    (iii) both those agreements are conditional upon the admission of the securities to the Official List of the Stock Exchange, and

    (iv) the consideration for each security is the same under both agreements,

and for these purposes 'newly subscribed securities' are securities which in pursuance of the arrangement referred to in (i) above, are issued wholly for new consideration.

This is intended to except from the stamp duty reserve tax the issue of renounceable letters of acceptance by an issuing house to applicants for shares in an offer for sale of new shares (see 44.1 above).

(*c*) An agreement if the securities to which the agreement relates are registered securities other than units under a unit trust scheme and

    (i) the agreement is made in pursuance of an offer to the public made by A,

    (ii) the agreement is conditional upon the admission of the securities to the Official List of the Stock Exchange, and

    (iii) under the agreement A issues to B or his nominee a renounceable letter of acceptance, or similar instrument, in respect of the securities.

This is intended to except from the stamp duty reserve tax the issue of renounceable letters of acceptance (by anyone, not just an issuing house) to applicants for shares in an offer for sale of existing registered shares (see 44.4 above).

Where it is sought to rely on one or more of the exceptions provided by *FA 1986, s 89A* care should be exercised to ensure that all the relevant conditions are met. For example, there is some doubt as to whether *FA 1986, s 89A(1)* can apply in a vendor placing due to uncertainty as to whether a vendor placing involves an 'offer to the public'.

45   Foreclosure

45.1 A foreclosure order is charged to ad valorem duty as a CONVEYANCE OR TRANSFER (28) on sale. [*SA, s 54; FA 1898, s 6*].

Ad valorem duty is not to be charged on a higher amount than the value of the property and if the value is stated in the order, that statement is conclusive for the calculation of ad valorem duty. The conveyance following the order is not liable to ad valorem duty if ad valorem duty has been paid on the order. [*FA 1898, s 6*].

46   Furnished Lettings

46.1 Duty is charged on furnished lettings under the head LEASES (53). It is as follows.

(*a*) Definite term of less than one year

(i) rent not exceeding £500—Nil,

(ii) rent exceeding £500—fixed duty £1.

(*b*) Term exceeding one year or indefinite—ad valorem duty on rent and premium. For details of rates of duty and what constitutes rent and length of term, see 53 LEASES.

46.2 An agreement for a furnished letting is liable as if it were an actual letting. [*SA, s 75(1)*]. See 5 AGREEMENT FOR LEASE.

47   Gifts

47.1 Ad valorem duty was charged by *F(1909–10)A 1910, s 74* on a CONVEYANCE OR TRANSFER (28) operating as a voluntary disposition inter vivos and calculated according to the value of the property conveyed; this charge was abolished by *FA 1985, s 82(1)*. However it was necessary to have the instrument stamped with a fixed 50p duty as a 'CONVEYANCE OR TRANSFER (28) of any kind not hereinbefore described' and to submit it for ADJUDICATION (2). [*FA 1985, s 82(5)*].

47.2 The *Stamp Duty (Exempt Instruments) Regulations 1987 (SI 1987 No 516)* now provide that a gift inter vivos which has been certified in accordance with the regulations is exempt from the fixed 50p duty and the requirement to submit it for ADJUDICATION (2). See 39 EXEMPT INSTRUMENTS.

The exemption does not apply to a sale at an undervalue nor to a gift of property subject to a debt. See 28 CONVEYANCE OR TRANSFER.

---

48   Goodwill

48.1 Goodwill is property for the purposes of stamp duty (e.g. *Potter v CIR Ex 1854, 10 Exch 147; Muller & Co's Margarine Ltd HL, [1901] AC 217*). Liability on a transfer of goodwill may be attracted

  (*a*) on sale (see 28 CONVEYANCE OR TRANSFER); or

  (*b*) on an AGREEMENT FOR SALE (6) under *SA, s 59*.

48.2 The following have been held liable to ad valorem duty:

  (*a*) an agreement for the sale of goodwill, existing independently of the property to which it relates (*West London Syndicate v CIR CA, [1898] 2 QB 507*); and

  (*b*) an agreement by a former proprietor not to operate a business in a specified area was held dutiable because it was equivalent to an agreement for the sale of goodwill (*Eastern National Omnibus Co v CIR KB 1938, [1939] 1 KB 161*).

48.3 Goodwill situated outside the UK will not attract duty if included in a sale agreement [*SA, s 59(1)*] (see 6.3 AGREEMENT FOR SALE), or in a CONVEYANCE OR TRANSFER (28) executed outside the UK [*SA, s 14(4)*] (see 20 CHARGEABILITY). For goodwill to be located outside the UK, both the business and the customers must be abroad (see *Benjamin Brooke & Co v CIR QB, [1896] 2 QB 356; Muller & Co's Margarine Ltd HL, [1901] AC 217*).

49   Instruments

49.1 Stamp duty is charged on instruments and not on individuals or transactions as such. [*SA, 1 Sch*].

'Instrument' is not fully defined, but includes every written document. [*SA, s 122(1)*]. The following provisions apply to instruments.

(*a*) They must be written in such a way that the stamp may appear on the face of the instrument and cannot be used for any other instrument written on the same piece of material. [*SA, s 3(1)*].

(*b*) More than one instrument may be written on the same piece of material but each instrument must be separately stamped with its own duty. [*SA, s 3(2)*]. A memorandum endorsed on an assurance policy to rectify a mistake in the original was a separate instrument liable to duty (*Prudential Assurance Co Ltd v CIR KB, [1935] 1 KB 101*).

(*c*) All the facts and circumstances affecting the liability to duty must be set out in the instrument. [*SA, s 5*].

49.2 STAMP DUTY RESERVE TAX (73) is charged not on instruments but on oral and written agreements to transfer chargeable securities (as defined) for a consideration in money or money's worth. The tax does not arise if an instrument transferring the securities to the purchaser is executed and duly stamped within two months of the agreement. [*FA 1986, s 87*].

49.3 For transactions that can be carried out without an instrument so as to avoid duty see 60 ORAL TRANSACTIONS.

50   Insurance Policies

50.1 Insurance and reinsurance policies are no longer liable to stamp duty. Since *FA 1970* only policies of life insurance or assurance had been liable to duty and this remaining charge was abolished for instruments made after 31 December 1989 by *FA 1989, s 173*.

50.2 **Assignments.** The assignment of an insurance policy may attract ad valorem duty as a CONVEYANCE OR TRANSFER (28) on sale (but see *Blandy v Herbert KB, (1829) 9 B & C 396* where no duty was payable on the assignment of a policy of marine insurance under which no loss had occurred; cf. *Western Abyssinian Mining Syndicate Ltd v CIR KB, (1935) 14 ATC 286*). Alternatively, a 50p duty may be attracted as a miscellaneous CONVEYANCE OR TRANSFER (28).

50.3 Declarations of trust of policy moneys, whether incorporated in any policy or executed separately, bear the 50p duty as a DECLARATION OF TRUST (31).

---

51   Ireland

51.1 NORTHERN IRELAND

Until 1974, stamp duties in Northern Ireland were charged by separate legislation and administered by the Minister of Finance for Northern Ireland. From 1 January 1974 (inclusive) the responsibility for administering stamp duties rests with the Commissioners of the Inland Revenue. (See the *Northern Ireland Constitution Act 1973, Northern Ireland Act 1974* and *SI 1973 No 2163*, and 3 ADMINISTRATION.)

Stamp duties prior to 1974 are found in Northern Ireland legislation. The duties charged are broadly the same as those described in this book but reference should be made to *SR & O 1922 No 80* (which applied *SA* and *SDMA*, as amended, to Northern Ireland) and subsequent *Finance (Northern Ireland) Acts*.

CAPITAL DUTY (18) was introduced for Northern Ireland in the same form as *FA 1973* and was abolished by *FA 1988, s 141*.

51.2 REPUBLIC OF IRELAND

The Republic has its own stamp duties and UK stamp duties do not extend to that country. See 51.3 below.

51.3 RELIEF FROM DOUBLE STAMP DUTY

Instruments chargeable with stamp duty in Great Britain, Northern Ireland and the Republic of Ireland are relieved from a double charge as follows.

(*a*) An instrument duly stamped in one country is deemed to be duly stamped to the extent of the duty it bears in the other country.

(*b*) But if a higher duty is charged in the other country the extra duty must be paid and denoted in the other country before it is duly stamped.

(*c*) Where duty is paid by way of composition in one country, an instrument is treated in the other country as duly stamped with the amount of duty which would have been chargeable but for the composition.

[*Government of Ireland Act 1920, s 29; SR & O 1923 No 406*].

52   Leading and Principal Object

52.1   It is a basic principle of stamp duty law that an instrument is stamped for its leading and principal object and this stamp covers incidental and accessory matters (see e.g. *Limmer Asphalte Paving Co v CIR Ex, (1872) LR 7 Ex 211*). Accordingly an exemption attaching to the leading and principal object should extend to any accessory matter.

52.2   If the instrument relates to *several distinct matters*, however, it is to be separately stamped for each matter. [*SA, s 4(a)*].

52.3   Separate stamps have been required, inter alia, in the following cases:

(a)   a lease with a contract for sale of fixtures (*Corder v Drakeford CP, (1811) 3 Taunt 382*);

(b)   an instrument providing for both the sale and sub-sale of shares (*Fitch Lovell Ltd v CIR Ch D, [1962] 3 All ER 685*);

(c)   an order which appointed new trustees to a charity and also vested the property in them (*Hadgett v CIR Ex D, (1877) 3 Ex D 46*);

(d)   an instrument whereby separate properties were leased to different lessees (*Doe d Copley v Day KB, (1811) 13 East 241*);

(e)   an instrument executed once as a lease and once as a conveyance on sale (*Brightman v CIR Ex, (1868) 18 LT 412*);

(f)   a lease containing an option to purchase separate property (*Lovelock v Franklyn QB, (1847) 8 QBR 371*);

(g)   an instrument comprising both a lease and a distinct agreement by another to pay penalties in case of the lessee's breach of an exclusive purchase covenant (*Wharton v Walton QB, (1845) 7 QB 474*).

52.4   Separate stamps have not been required, inter alia, in the following cases:

(a)   an instrument executed by more than one person where there is some common object or interest (e.g. *Baker v Jardine QB, (1784) 13 East 235n*);

(b)   a surrender of a lease and grant of new leases (*Doe d Phillipps v Phillipps QB, (1840) 11 Ad & E 796*);

(c)   a transfer by trustees to a life tenant following purchase of remainderman's interest stamped as a conveyance on sale of the interest but not as a transfer of the bare legal estate (*Oughtred v CIR HL, [1960] AC 206*);

(d)   a lease to joint tenants (*Cooper v Flynn CP(1), (1841) 3 Ir LR 472*);

(e)   a lease containing an option to the tenant to purchase the leased property (*Worthington v Warrington CP, (1848) 5 CB 635*; cf. *Lovelock v Franklyn* above);

(*f*) a lease containing a guarantee of the payment of rent (*Price v Thomas KB, (1831) 2 B & Ad 218*; cf. *Wharton v Walton* above).

52.5 An instrument made for any consideration which is chargeable to ad valorem duty is separately charged in respect of any other valuable consideration. [*SA, s 4(b)*]. For examples of the application of this see 53.4 LEASES; 24.3(*d*) COMPULSORY PURCHASE.

SA, s 4(b) can be excluded by express provisions, for example in relation to covenants to improve property (*FA 1900, s 10*, see 25.6 CONSIDERATION FOR SALE and *SA, s 77(2)*, see 53.6(*b*) LEASES and penal rents (*SA, s 77(1)*, see 53.5(*c*) LEASES)).

---

53   Leases

53.1 Stamp duty on leases is charged under the heading 'Lease or Tack'. [*SA, 1 Sch*]. The charge applies only to land, tenements or heritable subjects and does not extend to leases of personalty.

53.2 **A licence** does not attract stamp duty and must be distinguished from a lease. A licence does not give exclusive possession of the property (e.g. *Taylor v Caldwell QB, (1863) 3 B & S 826*). See *Jones v CIR QB, [1895] 1 QB 484* (agreement licensing installation of automatic washing machines not a lease); *Thames Conservators v CIR QB, (1886) 18 QBD 279* (licence to construct and retain a jetty not a lease); *Shell-Mex and BP v Manchester Garages CA, [1971] 1 All ER 841* (agreement in respect of a petrol station not a lease). See generally *Winter Garden Theatre (London) Ltd v Millennium Productions Ltd HL 1947, [1948] AC 173* and *Street v Mountford HL, [1985] AC 809*.

53.3 An AGREEMENT FOR LEASE (5) is charged to duty as a lease for the term and consideration provided in the agreement. [*SA, s 75(1); FA 1984, s 111(1)*]. Leases executed on or after 6 May 1994 must either contain a certificate to the effect that there was no prior agreement or be stamped with a stamp denoting either that the agreement is not chargeable with duty or the duty paid on the agreement. [*FA 1994, s 240*]. See also 5.3 AGREEMENT FOR LEASE.

53.4 Stamp duty is charged on both the rent and premium reserved in a lease (see 53.5 and 53.6 below). Where the instrument contains matters additional to

53.5 Leases

the grant of a lease, it is necessary to consider whether additional duties are payable. See 52 LEADING AND PRINCIPAL OBJECT.

A lease for no rent or premium and not in a form which attracts ad valorem duty under *FA 1994, ss 241* and *242* (see 53.5(*c*) and 53.6 (*e*), (*f*) below), attracts a fixed duty of £2.

53.5 DUTY ON RENT

[*SA, 1 Sch; FA 1974, 11 Sch 10; FA 1980, s 95(3); FA 1982, s 128(3)(4)*].

Since **21 March 1982** the rates of duty have been as follows.

(*a*) FURNISHED LETTINGS (46) for a definite term of less than one year bear no duty if the rent for the term does not exceed £500. Where the rent exceeds £500, duty of **£1** is charged.

(*b*) Any other lease for a definite term or any indefinite term bears duty as follows.

	Term of lease			
Yearly rent or average rate of rent	Not exceeding 7 years or indefinite	Exceeding 7 years but not exceeding 35 years	Exceeding 35 years but not exceeding 100 years	Exceeding 100 years
	£ p	£ p	£ p	£ p
Not exceeding £5 per annum.	Nil	0.10	0.60	1.20
Exceeding £5 and not exceeding £10.	Nil	0.20	1.20	2.40
Exceeding £10 and not exceeding £15.	Nil	0.30	1.80	3.60
Exceeding £15 and not exceeding £20.	Nil	0.40	2.40	4.80
Exceeding £20 and not exceeding £25.	Nil	0.50	3.00	6.00
Exceeding £25 and not exceeding £50.	Nil	1.00	6.00	12.00
Exceeding £50 and not exceeding £75.	Nil	1.50	9.00	18.00
Exceeding £75 and not exceeding £100.	Nil	2.00	12.00	24.00
Exceeding £100 and not exceeding £150.	Nil	3.00	18.00	36.00
Exceeding £150 and not exceeding £200.	Nil	4.00	24.00	48.00
Exceeding £200 and not exceeding £250.	Nil	5.00	30.00	60.00
Exceeding £250 and not exceeding £300.	Nil	6.00	36.00	72.00
Exceeding £300 and not exceeding £350.	Nil	7.00	42.00	84.00
Exceeding £350 and not exceeding £400.	Nil	8.00	48.00	96.00
Exceeding £400 and not exceeding £450.	Nil	9.00	54.00	108.00
Exceeding £450 and not exceeding £500.	Nil	10.00	60.00	120.00
Exceeding £500: for any full sum of £50 and also for any fractional part thereof.	0.50	1.00	6.00	12.00

[*SA 1891, 1 Sch*].

A lease for a definite term of less than a year bears duty as a lease for a year at the rent reserved for the term.

(*c*) '*Rent*' is not defined, but is generally a payment reserved out of the land (*Hill v Booth CA, [1930] 1 KB 381*) as recompense paid by the tenant to the landlord for exclusive possession. The wording used by the parties is not conclusive (*Donellan v Read KB, (1832) 3 B & Ad 899; Duke of Westminster v Store Properties Ltd Ch D, [1944] 1 Ch 129; Samuel v Salmon and Gluckstein Ltd Ch D 1945, [1946] Ch 8*).

Where a service charge is reserved as rent, it will bear duty as such (*Cox v Harper Ch D, [1910] 1 Ch 480*). If this additional payment is unascertained (e.g. a proportion of actual costs as determined from time to time) the fixed duty of £2 will be payable (in addition to any ad valorem duty in the basic rent).

Where the amount of the rent reserved is unascertained, but the lease specifies a maximum rent, that amount will attract duty under the CONTINGENCY PRINCIPLE (26) (*Coventry City Council v CIR Ch D, [1978] 1 All ER 1107*). Under the contingency principle, unascertained rent would also be subject to duty if only a minimum rent or basic rent subject to adjustment is stated in the lease. Where no maximum, minimum or basic rent is stated and the rent is otherwise unascertainable then the contingency principle does not apply and the rent is taken to be the market rent at that time and duty is charged accordingly. [*FA 1994, s 242(2)*]. See also 25.9 CONSIDERATION. See generally 26 CONTINGENCY PRINCIPLE.

Duty is not charged on penal rents reserved in a lease (additional rent payable in the case of the lessee's breach of covenant). [*SA, s 77(1)*].

See 78 VAT AND STAMP DUTY for the application of stamp duty where value added tax may be chargeable in relation to rent.

(*d*) **Term of lease**

(i) A lease for a specified period but terminable on an earlier event is treated as a lease for the specified period and not for an indefinite period (*Earl of Mount-Edgcumbe v CIR KB, [1911] 2 KB 24*; cf. *Kushner v Law Society KB, [1952] 1 KB 264*). Thus a lease for life or lives or for a term of years determinable on the marriage of the lessee treated as a lease for 90 years determinable on the death or marriage of the lessee under *Law of Property Act 1925, s 149(6)* is so treated for the purposes of stamp duty.

(ii) A lease or agreement granted for a fixed term and thereafter until determined is treated as a lease for a definite term equal to the fixed term plus any further period which must elapse before the earliest date at which the lease can be determined. [*FA 1963, s 56(3)*].

(iii) A lease for a term of years with an option to renew for a further specified period is charged to duty only on the original term (*Hand v Hall CA, (1877) LR 2 Ex D 355*).

(iv) Weekly or other periodic tenancies are probably the only examples of indefinite terms.

(v) The length of the lease is determined from the date of execution and any part of the term (and rent) in respect of the period prior to execution is ignored (see *Colton v Becollda Property Investments Ltd CA, [1950] 1 KB 216*).

(vi) Where on the grant of a lease the amount of the rent is ascertainable for part of the term and unascertainable for the remainder, the lease is treated as a lease for a term equal to the period for which the rent is ascertainable and duty is charged accordingly and the fixed duty of £2 is charged in respect of the remaining period for which the rent is unascertainable. No further duty can be charged when the rent for the remainder of the lease is finally ascertained, for example by rent review or according to an agreed formula. See Inland Revenue Statement (1963) *The Law Society's Gazette pp 175–6.* Following this statement the Commissioners will charge duty, for example, on a lease for a term of 101 years at a fixed rent for seven years with the rent for the remainder of the term to be agreed subsequently, as if the lease were a lease at the rate or average rate of rent for a seven-year term. The fixed duty of £2 will be charged in respect of the remainder of the lease. However, if there is a ground or peppercorn rent of a known amount for the entire term, ad valorem duty will be charged on the average ascertainable annual rent payable throughout the term and the fixed duty of £2 will be charged in respect of the unascertainable rent. It is not yet clear whether *FA 1994, s 242* will lead to a change in this practice and to stamp duty being charged on a market rent. See 53.5 (*c*) above. Arguably, a provision in the lease for a minimum rent should prevent this outcome.

53.6 **DUTY ON PREMIUMS**

[*SA, 1 Sch; FA 1994, s 241(5)*]

(*a*) Where part or all of the consideration for a lease for a definite term of more than one year or for an indefinite term consists of any money, stock, security or other property, duty is charged at the same rates as on a CONVEYANCE OR TRANSFER (28) on sale. The nil rate of duty applies if a CERTIFICATE OF VALUE (19) is included in the lease unless a part of the consideration includes rent exceeding £600 p.a. [*FA 1963, s 55(2); FA 1993, s 201(1)(b)*]. For valuation of the amount chargeable see 25 CONSIDERATION and (*e*) below.

(*b*) A lease granted for any consideration chargeable to ad valorem duty is not liable to duty in respect of any further consideration consisting of a covenant by the tenant to make a substantial improvement or addition to the leased property or a covenant relating to the matter of the lease. [*SA, s 77(2)*]. This exemption does not apply if the covenant would be chargeable with ad valorem duty if contained in a separate deed and the consideration is charged as a separate matter. [*Revenue Act 1909, s 8*].

(*c*) A premium is chargeable to duty if it consists of consideration moving either to the lessor or to any other person. This covers the case where a lease is granted to a builder's nominee and a premium is paid to the builder. (See also Revenue Statement August 1957 at 25.6 CONSIDERATION.)

(*d*) Sums paid to a lessor before the granting of a lease in respect of the costs of works to meet the lessee's particular needs are dutiable as a premium.

(*e*) For leases executed after 7 December 1993 duty is charged not only when the premium consists of money, stock or securities but also when it consists of any other property. [*FA 1994, s 241(5)*]. This means that on a sale and lease back transaction consisting of the sale of the freehold in consideration of the grant of a new lease back stamp duty will be charged as follows:

(i) on the freehold sale with reference to the market value of the lease back; and

(ii) on the lease back with reference to the market value of the freehold.

(*f*) Where the premium in whole or in part cannot be ascertained when the lease is granted, it is taken to be the market value of the lease on a sale in the open market at that time and duty is charged accordingly. [*FA 1994, s 242(1)*]. The CONTINGENCY PRINCIPLE (26) will however take precedence where there is a maximum, minimum or basic figure. See 25.9 CONSIDERATION.

53.7 SURRENDERS AND VARIATIONS

(*a*) No duty is charged on a lease or agreement made in consideration for the surrender or abandonment of an existing lease relating to the same property. [*SA, s 77(1)*]. It is understood that the Stamp Office accept that this continues to be the position notwithstanding *FA 1994, s 241* which arguably would impose an ad valorem charge to duty on the market value of the property immediately before the grant of the lease.

(*b*) Where a lease is surrendered, duty is payable on any consideration paid by the landlord (but not on any consideration paid by the tenant to the landlord) as a CONVEYANCE OR TRANSFER (28) on sale. Where the consideration for the surrender consists of the grant of a new lease of a different property the surrender used to attract only a fixed 50p duty under the head SURRENDER (74). However, *FA 1994, s 241* creates an ad valorem charge to duty on the surrender of a lease in consideration of the grant of a new lease of the same or a different property. The duty is charged with reference to the market value of the new lease. The new lease will itself attract stamp duty on any premium and rent and the value of the surrendered lease unless the new lease is of the same property when the value of the surrendered lease will be ignored under *SA, s 77(1)* (and see 53.7(*a*) above). No duty can be charged where there is no stampable instrument such as a deed of surrender, memorandum or receipt. Surrender by operation of law, where the landlord pays the tenant and in exchange receives the keys and the lease, avoids duty because there is nothing to stamp. However, a written agreement to surrender a lease made after 7 December 1993 where there is no deed of surrender, is treated as a deed of surrender and is chargeable and chargeable to duty accordingly. [*FA 1994, s 243*].

(*c*) Where the terms of a lease can only be varied by a surrender and regrant (e.g. the lengthening of the term), the regranted lease bears the appropriate duty but no extra duty is paid on the surrendered lease. It is understood that the Stamp Office do not seek to charge duty on the surrender with reference to the market value of the new lease under *FA 1994, s 241*. However, where there is a written agreement to surrender

FA 1994, s 243 may apply to charge ad valorem duty on any cash consideration paid by the landlord.

(d) The withdrawal by mutual agreement of a notice to determine a tenancy constitutes a new tenancy liable to ad valorem duty (*Tayleur v Wildin Ex, (1868) L R 3 Exch 303; Freeman v Evans CA, [1922] 1 Ch 36*).

(e) A variation which does not operate as a surrender and regrant is not charged under the heading 'Lease' but may attract duty under some other head.

(f) An instrument increasing the rent under a lease, not being a surrender and regrant and liable to duty as in 53.7(c) above, attracts duty under the head 'Bond, Covenant' (see 16 BONDS) but the duty is calculated as Lease duty on the additional rent. (*Gable Construction Co Ltd v CIR Ch D, [1968] 2 All ER 968*) [*SA, s 77(5); FA 1971, s 64(1)(a)*]. An instrument agreeing an increased rent by reference to a formula in a lease is not, however, chargeable with ad valorem duty unless it operates as a regrant (53.7(c) above).

53.8 SHARED OWNERSHIP LEASES

The usual rules for calculating duty on leases are varied for certain types of lease granted by a local housing authority, registered or unregistered housing association, housing action trust, development corporation, the Commission for the New Towns and some similar bodies. [*FA 1980, s 97; FA 1981, s 108; FA 1987, s 54; FA 1988, s 142*]. In a shared ownership scheme the tenant purchases part of his council house, pays rent for the remainder and is given an option to acquire the reversion. The tenant is permitted to pay ad valorem duty once under the CONVEYANCE OR TRANSFER (28) on sale head on the market value of the house instead of paying duty first under the lease head and second, when he acquires the reversion. A private sector landlord who has acquired a council housing estate is also included in these provisions so that a tenant may insist on a shared ownership lease even though his council estate has been bought by a private landlord. *Sec 97* applies

(a) where the lease is of a dwelling for the exclusive use of the lessee (or joint lessees);

(b) where the lease is granted partly in consideration of a premium calculated by reference to the market value of the dwelling or a sum calculated by reference to that value and partly in consideration of rent;

(c) where the lease provides for the lessee to acquire the reversion; and in addition states the market value or the sum referred to in (b) above and a statement that the parties intend duty to be charged in accordance with *Sec 97* by reference to that sum.

The stamp duty consequences are then as follows:

(i) when the lease is granted duty is payable under the CONVEYANCE OR TRANSFER (28) on sale head as if it were a conveyance in consideration of the amount mentioned in the lease as in (*b*) above and no duty is payable under the lease head;

(ii) an instrument executed in pursuance of the lease on which duty has been paid as in (i) (and containing a statement to that effect), whereby the reversion is transferred to the lessee, bears no duty.

53.9 CHARITIES

Leases granted to charities are not chargeable with duty, although it is necessary to have the lease adjudicated. [*FA 1982, s 129*]. See ADJUDICATION (2).

53.10 CROWN EXEMPTION

Leases granted to a Government Minister or to the Treasury Solicitor are not chargeable with duty. [*FA 1987, s 55*].

53.11 PRODUCED STAMP

A lease or AGREEMENT FOR LEASE (5) for a term of seven years or more must be not only stamped but also 'produced' to the Commissioners and stamped with a PRODUCED STAMP (66). A lease granted pursuant to and consistent with a produced agreement for a lease need not itself be produced. [*FA 1931, s 28(2)*].

52.12 LEASES BETWEEN ASSOCIATED COMPANIES

Because stamp duty on leases is charged under the head 'Lease or Tack', the exemption for transfers between ASSOCIATED COMPANIES (12) under *FA 1930, s 42* does not apply. However, for instruments executed on or after 1 May 1995, *FA 1995, s 151* exempts leases, agreements for leases and 'agreements with respect to a letting' between associated companies from duty subject to the requirements of that section. See 12.8 ASSOCIATED COMPANIES.

---

54   Letters of Allotment and Acceptance

54.1 STAMP DUTY

The head of charge Letters of Allotment or Renunciation, Scrip Certificates or Scrip in *SA, 1 Sch* was abolished by *FA 1949*. The instruments formerly charged were

(*a*) letter of allotment and letter of renunciation of shares in or of loans raised by a company, municipal body or corporation (including overseas bodies and governments where issued in the UK);

54.2 Letters of Allotment and Acceptance

(b) scrip certificates or scrip entitling any person to become the proprietor of any share in or denoting the right of any person as a subscriber in respect of any loan raised by a company, municipal body or corporation (including overseas bodies and governments where issued or delivered in the UK). See 71 SCRIP DIVIDENDS.

54.2 Renounceable letters of allotment and acceptance where the rights are renounceable not later than six months after issue are also exempt from duty under the BEARER INSTRUMENTS (13) head of charge. [*SA, 1 Sch*]. There is also a general exemption for such letters from duty under the CONVEYANCE OR TRANSFER (28) on sale head although this exemption is no longer available in relation to company takeovers where the 'Pref-trick' could otherwise be used to avoid stamp duty on the transfer of the company. [*FA 1963, s 65(1); FA 1985, s 81*]. See 13.7(b) BEARER INSTRUMENTS.

54.3 The previous exemption from duty under the BEARER INSTRUMENTS (13) head for bearer letters of allotment, bearer letters of rights, scrip and scrip certificates to bearer required to be surrendered not later than six months after issue, has been withdrawn. [*FA 1986, s 80*].

54.4 STAMP DUTY RESERVE TAX (73). The exemptions from stamp duty for renounceable letters of allotment and acceptance and similar instruments where the rights are renounceable not later than six months after issue do not protect such instruments from the STAMP DUTY RESERVE TAX (73) charge on agreements to transfer such instruments for money or money's worth. The structure of the tax is such that the exemption from bearer instrument duty results automatically in a tax charge on short-term renounceable letters of allotment and acceptance because there can be no stamped instrument. [*FA 1986, ss 87(1)(2), 88 (2)(3)*].

54.5 For a more detailed description of the tax charge on agreements to transfer short-term renounceable letters of allotment and acceptance see 73 STAMP DUTY RESERVE TAX. For an explanation of the situations in which the tax will normally arise see 44 FLOTATIONS, ETC.

---

55 Loan Capital and Debentures

Note. The stamp duty and stamp duty reserve tax charges in relation to loan capital were to be abolished from a date to be appointed by statutory instrument. [*FA 1990, ss 108–111*]. But see 1.1 INTRODUCTION.

55.1 As a result of the exemptions from duty for both bearer and registered loan capital under *FA 1986, s 79* and the abolition of the duty on the transfer of debentures by *FA 1971, s 64* most types of loan capital are exempt from stamp duty.

55.2 *Loan capital* is defined as

'(*a*) any debenture stock, corporation stock or funded debt, by whatever name known, issued by a body corporate or other body of persons (which here includes a local authority and any body whether formed or established in the UK or elsewhere);

(*b*) any capital raised by such a body if the capital is borrowed or has the character of borrowed money, and whether it is in the form of stock or any other form;

(*c*) stock or marketable securities issued by the government of any country or territory outside the United Kingdom.'

[*FA 1986, ss 78(7), 79(12)*].

This definition is similar to that used for the former head of charge 'Loan Capital' (abolished by *FA 1973*) and cases decided under that head are therefore relevant to the current definition. In *Reed International Ltd v CIR HL, [1975] 3 All ER 218* it was held that 'funded debt' requires the characteristics of long-term borrowing but does not have to be created out of existing debt; in *A-G v South Wales Electrical Power Distribution Co CA, [1920] 1 KB 552* it was held that interest-bearing deferred warrants issued by a company in respect of the unpaid interest due on its debenture stock was not 'loan capital' or 'funded debt' and not 'borrowed money' because it was not of a capital nature; in *A-G v Regents Canal and Dock Co CA, [1904] 1 KB 263* it was held that new debenture stock issued following the extinction of existing debenture stock was 'loan capital'—new money is not required.

It is thought that short-term debt of a capital nature is within the definition of loan capital and will therefore also qualify for the following exemptions.

55.3 **Bearer loan capital** is exempt from duty under the BEARER INSTRUMENTS (13) head on issue and on transfer. [*FA 1986, s 79(2)*].

55.4 **Registered loan capital.** Transfers of most types of registered loan capital are exempt from duty under the head CONVEYANCE OR TRANSFER (28) on sale. [*FA 1986, s 79(3)(4)*]. The exemption does not apply to

(*a*) an instrument transferring loan capital which, at the time it is executed, carries a right, exercisable then or later, of conversion into shares or other securities, or to the acquisition of shares or other securities including loan capital of the same description; or

(*b*) an instrument transferring loan capital which at the time it is executed or any earlier time carries or has carried

(i) a right to interest exceeding a reasonable commercial return on the nominal amount of capital,

(ii) a right to interest the amount of which is determined by reference to the results of a business or the value of property, or

(iii) a right on repayment to an amount which exceeds the nominal amount of the capital and is not reasonably comparable with what is generally repayable on loan capital listed on The Stock Exchange.

The fact that the interest or the amount repayable is index-linked does not prevent the exemption from applying. [*FA 1986, s 79(7)*].

In relation to (*a*) above, loan capital is not excluded from the exemption because it carries an unexpired right of conversion into or acquisition of loan capital which itself comes within the terms of the exemption (Statement of Practice 3/84 which originally applied to *FA 1976, s 126* but continues to apply to the exemption now contained in *FA 1986, s 79*).

Where the transfer of registered loan capital is not exempt duty is charged at the rate of 50p for every £100 or part of £100 of the amount or value of the consideration for the transfer under the head CONVEYANCE OR TRANSFER (28) on sale.

55.5 DEBENTURES

Debentures are normally exempt from duty under the above-mentioned provisions. A further exemption is available by reason of the abolition of the Mortgage, Bond, Debenture, Covenant head of charge including the charge on the transfer of debentures other than marketable securities. [*FA 1971, s 64(1)*]. It follows from this that the transfer of debentures which are not marketable securities will be exempt from duty [*FA 1971, s 64(2)*] (see 57.3 MORTGAGES). The debentures of a private company are not marketable securities. [*Financial Services Act 1986, s 170*]. A debenture has been defined as a written instrument creating, acknowledging or evidencing indebtedness (*Levy v Abercorris Slate Slab Co Ch D, (1888) 37 Ch D 260*) and there is judicial support for the view that a bank facility letter can be a debenture even though no money has been drawn down at the time (*NV Slavenburg's Bank v Intercontinental Natural Resources Ltd Ch D, [1980] 1 WLR 1076*).

---

56   Manner of Stamping

56.1 DENOTING OF DUTY

Stamp duties are generally denoted on the instruments to which they relate by an impressed stamp. [*SA, s 2*].

56.2 See 49 INSTRUMENTS for how stamps should appear on instruments.

56.3 See 63 PAYMENT OF DUTY OR TAX for details of dates of stamping and liability for duty and penalties.

56.4 *FA 1993, s 204* has given the Treasury wide powers to make regulations as to the manner by which stamp duty is denoted. The regulations may for example provide for duty to be denoted by the traditional impressed stamp, by adhesive stamp or by computer record.

57 Mortgages

57.1 Stamp duty formerly charged by *SA, 1 Sch* on mortgages was abolished by *FA 1971, s 64(1)(c), 14 Sch.*

57.2 The documents formerly charged were mortgages and similar documents of the following descriptions,

(*a*) the principal or primary security under a legal mortgage for the payment or repayment of money;

(*b*) a collateral or substituted security under a legal mortgage;

(*c*) an equitable mortgage;

(*d*) a transfer or assignment of a mortgage or any money or stock secured by a mortgage;

(*e*) a reconveyance or release or similar instrument of a mortgage or the money secured thereby.

57.3 Instruments formerly charged under the head 'Mortgage' will not attract duty under any other head. For example, that head of charge included a charge on the transfer of debentures other than marketable securities and the abolition of that charge does not permit duty to be charged under the head CONVEYANCE OR TRANSFER (28) on sale. [*FA 1971, s 64(2)*]. (See 55 LOAN CAPITAL AND DEBENTURES.) However, an instrument containing several distinct matters (see 52 LEADING AND PRINCIPAL OBJECT) will only be exempt to the extent that a matter falls within the former head of charge.

57.4 **Transfer of property subject to a mortgage.** See 25 CONSIDERATION FOR SALE.

58   Negotiating with the Stamp Office

58.1   Most stampable documents are stamped over the counter at one of the offices listed in 3.4 and 3.5 ADMINISTRATION following a cursory examination of the document by one of the marking clerks. Documents stamped in this way are not guaranteed to be correctly stamped. Consequently, a registrar may properly refuse to register such a document stamped in this way if it appears that it does not bear the correct stamp. Alternatively, the person presenting the document for stamping over the counter may disagree with the marker about the stamp duty liability and decline to stamp it at that stage. In either case it is open to the registrar or the person wishing to stamp the document to request that the document be adjudicated. ADJUDICATION (2) is the process whereby the Stamp Office formally assesses the amount of duty, if any, chargeable on the document. Except in the cases mentioned in 2.5 above, adjudication is conclusive of the liability of the document to stamp duty. [*SA, s 12(5)*]. In addition to disputes about the liability of a document to stamp duty, adjudication is used where it is not possible to determine the liability of a document to stamp duty without detailed consideration. This occurs most commonly with sales when a set of accounts or a property valuation is required or the consideration clause in a sale document contains complicated financial formulae or legal wording. In these cases the usual practice is to submit the document direct to the Stamp Office at Worthing (see 3.3 above) for adjudication. When a valuation is required, the Stamp Office may refer to specialist valuers in other departments. Adjudication is also used in order to decide whether a document qualifies for a specific exemption or relief from stamp duty, such as those available for COMPANY REORGANISATIONS (23).

58.2   Following the submission of the document for adjudication the Stamp Office examines it and issues stamps form ADJ 407 to the applicant. This form contains a statement of the amount of stamp duty payable based on the information supplied to the Stamp Office. Following the issue of form ADJ 407, the stamp duty will either be paid or the applicant for adjudication will normally write back explaining that, in his opinion, the duty payable is wrong and discussions will then ensue leading, usually, to agreement of the amount of duty payable.

The following notice appeared in The Law Society's Gazette of 18 July 1990:

'The Stamp Office has announced an administrative modification to its adjudication procedures. Following examination of an instrument for adjudication, the Stamp Office's practice is to notify the applicant of the amount of duty estimated to be payable. Normally, this leads to one of two courses of action: the applicant either agrees and remits the duty, or notifies the stamp office of his disagreement. If the applicant agrees, the instrument is stamped and returned; if he disagrees, discussions by way of correspondence between the applicant and the office may follow with the aim of reaching agreement or, where necessary, a formal assessment is issued.

Sometimes, however, there is no response at all from the applicant to the Stamp Office's estimate—no payment of duty or indication of disagreement. Nevertheless, duty is normally eventually paid, but it may be necessary for the Stamp Office to issue a number of reminders. This is administratively inconvenient and wasteful of the Office's resources.

The Office has therefore introduced a change in procedure. It will continue to allow 28 days for applicants to respond to estimates of duty payable. If no response has been received after 28 days, a reminder will be issued, but this will be the only reminder. The Office will consider the request for adjudication as having been withdrawn once a further 14 days have elapsed after the issue of the reminder, and will then return the instrument unstamped to the applicant.

This will not prevent the applicant from representing the instrument for adjudication. However, *section 14(4)* (instrument not duly stamped not to be given in evidence) and *section 15* (penalty upon stamping instruments after execution) of the *Stamp Act 1891* might apply in that event of delay.'

The precise status of form ADJ 407 is not entirely clear. Form ADJ 407 is probably not an 'assessment' for the purposes of *SA, s 15(2)(b)* because the amount of stamp duty shown on the form is tentative and subject to the agreement of the applicant. This argument is given further credence when one considers that what is usually referred to as the *formal assessment* is only issued by the Stamp Office when an appeal to the High Court is in prospect.

The conclusion to be drawn from this is that so long as the document to be adjudicated is lodged within thirty days there will in practice never be any question of penalties (unless the document is returned to the applicant and later resubmitted). This is because an 'assessment' is never actually issued except where there will be an appeal to the High Court. At first sight this situation may appear rather odd to someone who is used to the rigorous penalty rules which apply to delayed payment of income tax, corporation tax, capital gains tax and value added tax. On the other hand, it can be said that this situation is entirely in keeping with the voluntary nature of stamp duty and the structure of the 1891 Act.

58.3   The discussions with the Stamp Office which often occur following the issue of stamps form ADJ 407 are a very important practical stage in settling the liability of the document to stamp duty. Such discussions may extend over a considerable time (a year or more is not unusual) with the applicant for adjudication not having to part with any money until such time as he agrees the liability to stamp duty. Although the opportunity to engage in negotiations with the Stamp Office in this way is not expressly provided for in SA, such negotiations reflect the voluntary nature of stamp duty and the consequent absence of any power by the Stamp Office to enforce payment except in the case of duty under the BEARER INSTRUMENTS (13) head.

58.4   In practice, the Stamp Office tries to be helpful during negotiations and is usually prepared to exchange correspondence several times with the applicant or his advisers where an important legal point is involved so long as the applicant is arguing in good faith and is not seeking merely to defer payment of the duty. Very often the adjudication officer will support his view of the liability to stamp duty by quoting from the current edition of Sergeant and Sims on Stamp Duties. This book, currently in its tenth edition, is well known and has almost the status of an official stamp duty manual so far as the Stamp Office is concerned, having been written by a member of the legal advisory staff of the Inland Revenue. The applicant for adjudication should always quote to the Stamp Office any passage from Sergeant and Sims which he can find in support of his case, since such statements will carry considerable weight with the adjudication officer. A useful example of such a passage is the second complete paragraph on page 374 of the tenth edition of Sergeant and Sims which can be of help when applying for exemption from stamp duty under *FA 1930, s 42* (see 12 ASSOCIATED COMPANIES). If the adjudication officer and the applicant cannot agree the liability on the basis of arguments put forward by the officer on his own, it is usual for the officer to seek the views of a specialist in the solicitors department of the Inland Revenue. If the solicitors department confirm the adjudication officer's view of the stamp duty liability, the applicant for adjudication will normally be faced with paying the duty or commencing a formal appeal to the High Court under *SA, s 13* (see 9 APPEALS) or withdrawing his document from the adjudication.

---

59   Options and Equity Warrants

59.1 STAMP DUTY

There is no head of charge specifically for options. Options may be chargeable under the head CONVEYANCE OR TRANSFER (28) on sale, the miscellaneous conveyance or transfer head or the BEARER INSTRUMENTS (13) head unless any of the exemptions listed in 59.6 below applies.

59.2 CONVEYANCE OR TRANSFER (28)

An agreement creating an option to purchase land has been held to attract ad valorem duty as a conveyance on sale on the grounds that (i) the option was property or an interest in property, (ii) the instrument creating the option vested property or an interest in property (namely the option) in the purchaser and (iii) the agreement was therefore a conveyance on sale as defined in *SA, s 54* (see 28.4 CONVEYANCE OR TRANSFER). (*George Wimpey & Co Ltd v CIR CA, [1975] 2 All ER 45*). Instruments granting put or call or put and call options may therefore attract ad valorem duty at £1 per £100 or part of £100 of the consideration unless the option is a marketable security in which case the reduced rate of 50p per £100 or part of £100 applies. A

CERTIFICATE OF VALUE (19) may be given where appropriate but such a certificate is not available where the option is a marketable security.

59.3 LEASES (53)

A lease of land containing an option to purchase the freehold does not require to be stamped in relation to the option unless the option relates to separate property. (*Worthington v Warrington, (1848) 5 CB 635; Lovelock v Franklyn, (1846) 8 QB 371*).

59.4 AGREEMENT FOR SALE (6)

An agreement for the sale of a subsisting option to purchase a legal interest is thought to be liable under *SA, s 59* as either an agreement for the sale of an equitable interest or an agreement for the sale of an estate or interest in property not falling within one of the specified exemptions (see 6 AGREEMENT FOR SALE). (See *George Wimpey & Co Ltd v CIR* above; *Muller & Co's Margarine Ltd v CIR CA, [1900] 1 QB 310* explained in *Danubian Sugar Factories Ltd v CIR CA, [1901] 1 KB 245*.) However, an agreement for the sale of a legal interest in land with an option to take a declaration of trust is not an agreement for the sale of an equitable interest in land (*West London Syndicate v CIR CA, [1898] 2 QB 507*) and an agreement granting an option to purchase coupled with an immediate transfer of shares, no beneficial interest passing, was not liable under *Sec 59* (*Wm Cory & Son Ltd v CIR HL, [1965] AC 1088*).

59.5 BEARER OPTIONS

If the instrument granting the option is a bearer instrument it may attract duty on issue or on first transfer in the UK under the BEARER INSTRUMENTS (13) head of charge. [*FA 1963, s 59(2)(4)*]. The transfer by delivery of an existing bearer option will not attract duty.

59.6 EXEMPTIONS

A put or call option is exempt from stamp duty under the heads mentioned above if it relates to

(*a*) gilt-edged securities;

(*b*) exempt loan capital (see 55 LOAN CAPITAL AND DEBENTURES);

(*c*) debentures which are not marketable securities;

(*d*) bearer securities relating to stock expressed in any currency except sterling or in units of account defined by reference to more than one currency (see 13 BEARER INSTRUMENTS).

[*FA 1987, s 50; F(No 2)A 1987, s 99*].

59.7 EQUITY WARRANTS

Instead of issuing convertible loan stock a borrower may issue loan stock with warrants to subscribe for shares in the borrower or another company.

59.8 Options and Equity Warrants

These equity warrants may be detached from the loan stock and traded separately in the market. When detached from the loan stock the equity warrant will attract stamp duty in the manner described above in relation to options.

Transfers of loan stock with equity warrants attached may not qualify for the general exemption from stamp duty for transfers of registered loan capital by reason of the loan stock carrying the right of conversion into shares. [*FA 1986, s 79(4)(5)*]. See 55 LOAN CAPITAL AND DEBENTURES.

59.8 STAMP DUTY RESERVE TAX (72)

An option to acquire stocks or shares which are not themselves exempt from stamp duty on transfer is a 'chargeable security' for the purposes of the tax. The same applies to an option to acquire loan capital. [*FA 1986, s 99(3)(c); FA 1988, s 144(2)*]. See 73.7. Therefore, an agreement to transfer an existing call option or equity warrant in registered form relating to stocks or shares or loan capital which are not themselves exempt from stamp duty will attract tax unless a duly stamped instrument of transfer is produced within two months of the agreement.

The issue of such a call option or equity warrant may also attract tax under the principle established in *George Wimpey & Co Ltd v CIR CA, [1975] 2 All ER 45* (see 59.2 above). However, it has been argued that the grant of an option although constituting a conveyance of the option is not actually an 'agreement' to transfer as required by the *FA 1986, s 87(1)* and the Stamp Office apparently accepts this. A put option is not a 'chargeable security' for the purposes of the tax because it is an option enabling the holder to sell rather than to acquire stocks or shares or loan capital.

Options in bearer form, except renounceable LETTERS OF ALLOTMENT AND ACCEPTANCE (54) where the rights are renounceable not later than six months after issue, are outside the scope of the tax. [*FA 1986, s 90(3)*].

---

60 Oral Transactions

60.1 Stamp duty is charged on INSTRUMENTS (49). Transactions which are done by word of mouth or physical delivery are not liable to duty. Duty may thus be avoided when a transaction is carried out orally instead of being reduced to writing. However, in relation to oral agreements to transfer 'chargeable securities' for money or money's worth STAMP DUTY RESERVE TAX (73) will apply unless an instrument transferring the securities to the purchaser is executed and duly stamped within two months of the agreement.

60.2 Transactions that can be effected orally include the following.

(*a*) The transfer of various types of personalty by delivery such as stock in trade, jewellery, furniture, plant and machinery and fixtures (after severance).

(*b*) A written agreement for the sale of 'goods, wares and merchandise' does not attract duty under *SA, s 59* (see 6 AGREEMENT FOR SALE) and subsequent completion of the transaction by delivery as in (*a*) above will avoid duty. This means that the consideration for the goods etc. is left out of account in deciding whether a CERTIFICATE OF VALUE (19) is appropriate.

(*c*) BEARER INSTRUMENTS (13) can pass by delivery and so do not attract duty on transfer.

(*d*) Oral declarations of trust of personalty (see 75 TRUSTS AND TRUSTEES).

It will often be desirable to have a written record of a transaction that has been carried out orally. The written record may be treated as one with the oral transaction and stampable as an instrument effecting the transaction (*Cohen and Moore v CIR KB, [1933] 2 KB 126*). However, a written record of the transaction which is brought into existence not for the purpose of recording the transaction but to fulfil a legal requirement such as a board minute prepared pursuant to *Companies Act 1985, s 382* is not vulnerable under the rule in *Cohen and Moore* and is not therefore stampable. Moreover, a memorandum prepared before the transaction occurs cannot be liable to duty because liability depends on the facts and circumstances which exist at the date of the document.

60.3 The following transactions, inter alia, require a written instrument:

(*a*) the conveyance of land [*Law of Property Act 1925, s 52*];

(*b*) the disposition of an equitable interest [*Law of Property Act 1925, s 53*];

(*c*) the transfer of shares in a company subject to regulations to be made under *Companies Act 1989, s 207* which will enable title to securities to be evidenced and transferred without a written instrument [*Companies Act 1985, s 183(1)(2)*].

See 72 SHARES AND SECURITIES.

An attempted oral disposition of an equitable interest has been held ineffective with the result that a subsequent declaration of trust was stampable as a CONVEYANCE OR TRANSFER (28) (*Grey v CIR HL 1959, [1960] AC 1*). See 75 TRUSTS AND TRUSTEES.

61 Overseas Matters

61.1 CHARGE TO STAMP DUTY

Stamp duty applies to

(a) any instrument executed in the UK even if it relates to property outside the UK; and

(b) any instrument executed outside the UK that relates to any property in the UK, or to any matter or thing done or to be done in the UK. For the consequences of failing to stamp see *SA, s 14(4)* and 20 CHARGEABILITY.

For stamp duty the UK comprises England, Scotland, Wales and Northern Ireland but not the Channel Islands nor the Isle of Man. The territorial extension of the UK to the continental shelf by *ICTA 1988, s 830* for the purposes of income tax and corporation tax does not apply to stamp duty.

61.2 INSTRUMENTS EXECUTED ABROAD

The payment of duty on an instrument executed abroad and relating to UK matters is deferred until the instrument is received in the UK. See 63 PAYMENT OF DUTY OR TAX.

61.3 FOREIGN CURRENCY

Where the consideration is expressed in a foreign currency it is converted at the rate current at the date of the instrument. See 25 CONSIDERATION.

61.4 OVERSEAS COMPANY

An overseas company may be an associated company for the purpose of the ASSOCIATED COMPANIES (12) relief. The reliefs for COMPANY REORGANISATIONS (23) are not available unless the registered office of the acquiring company is in the UK.

61.5 OVERSEAS BRANCH REGISTERS

The transfer of a share registered in an overseas branch register (other than a register in Northern Ireland) is deemed to be a transfer of non-UK property and unless executed in the UK the transfer is exempt from stamp duty. [*Companies Act 1985, s 362, 14 Sch 8*]. See 61.7 below.

61.6 BEARER INSTRUMENTS

BEARER INSTRUMENTS (13) relating to stock expressed in any currency other than sterling or in any units of account defined by reference to more than one currency are exempt from duty under the head 'Bearer Instrument'.

61.7 STAMP DUTY RESERVE TAX

The legislation does not contain any provision setting out the territorial scope of the tax. The principles which apply for stamp duty (see 61.1 above) have no application because the tax is not a stamp duty. In the absence of such a provision the territorial scope is likely to depend upon the power of the Commissioners to raise an assessment on non-UK resident purchasers. The Commissioners are empowered to assess non-resident purchasers in the name of a branch or agent. [*The Stamp Duty Reserve Tax Regulations 1986 (SI 1986 No 1711), para 20* applying and modifying *Taxes Management Act 1970, s 78*]. The concept of 'fiscal presence' which governs the territorial scope of the requirement for an employer to operate the 'pay as you earn' (PAYE) system of deduction of income tax may apply by analogy. [*ICTA 1988, s 203*]. (See *Clark v Oceanic Contractors Inc HL, [1983] 2 WLR 94*.)

62   Partnerships

62.1 FORMATION OF PARTNERSHIPS

A partnership deed or agreement as such does not attract any stamp duty. Before the repeal of the Deeds head of charge an instrument under seal attracted a fixed duty of 50p. [*FA 1985, s 85, 24 Sch (e)*]. A limited partnership was a 'capital company' for the purposes of CAPITAL DUTY (18) and as such was within the charge to duty. This duty has been abolished. [*FA 1988, s 141*]. Limited partnerships remain liable to stamp duty as before.

62.2 INCOMING PARTNERS

If a new partner pays money direct to existing partners in return for an interest in the partnership property any document transferring the interest to the new partner will attract ad valorem duty as a CONVEYANCE OR TRANSFER (28) on sale of the interest in the partnership property purchased by the new partner. However, if the new partner contributes cash equal to the amount credited to his capital account no ad valorem duty is chargeable unless there is a simultaneous withdrawal of capital by an existing or retiring partner in which case the document effecting the transaction is treated as a CONVEYANCE OR TRANSFER (28) on sale and is chargeable to duty as such.

62.3 DISSOLUTION OF PARTNERSHIP

The division of assets on a dissolution of partnership in accordance with the terms of the partnership will not normally attract ad valorem duty (*Macleod v CIR Ex(S) 1885, 22 Sc LR 674*). The instrument effecting a dissolution will, however, attract a fixed 50p duty under the head 'Partition'. (See 37 EXCHANGE OR PARTITION.) If there is an element of sale in the dissolution, ad valorem duty may be charged on the dissolution instrument as a CONVEYANCE

62.4 Partnerships

OR TRANSFER (28) on sale (*Christie v CIR Ex, (1866) LR 2 Ex 46; Garnett v CIR QB 1899, 81 LT 633*).

62.4 CONVERSION TO A COMPANY

Where the business of a partnership is transferred to a company, the transfers of assets to the company are charged to ad valorem duty as a CONVEYANCE OR TRANSFER (28) on sale, notwithstanding that the partners are the same persons as the owners of shares in the company (*Foster (John) & Sons v CIR CA, [1894] 1 QB 516*).

---

63 Payment of Duty or Tax

63.1 DATE OF STAMPING AND PAYMENT

(*a*) General. Except for the instruments considered below, an instrument should be stamped before execution. In practice, the Commissioners permit stamping within 30 days without the general penalty mentioned below unless there are specific penalty provisions (see 64 PENALTIES AND OFFENCES). An unstamped or insufficiently-stamped instrument may otherwise be stamped after execution on payment of the unpaid duty, a penalty of £10 and, where the duty exceeds £10, interest at 5% p.a. from the date of execution (with a maximum of the unpaid duty). [*SA, s 15(1)*].

(*b*) Certain instruments chargeable with ad valorem duty, being those charged under the following heads

AGREEMENT FOR LEASE (5)

CLEARANCE SERVICES (22)

CONVEYANCE OR TRANSFER (28) on sale

DEPOSITARY RECEIPTS (34)

LEASES (53)

unless written on stamped material, must be stamped with the proper ad valorem duty within 30 days of first execution. However, if the Commissioners have been asked to express an opinion on the amount of duty (see 2 ADJUDICATION) *within that time*, duty is payable within 14 days of the assessment. Thus requesting that a document be adjudicated can defer payment of duty until after an assessment is issued. Instruments which are not properly stamped within these time limits incur a fine of £10 and a penalty as in (*a*) above *and* unless there is a reasonable excuse for the delay in stamping or an insufficiency of stamp, a further penalty equivalent to the duty may be charged. [*SA, s 15(2); FA 1984, s 111(4)(5); FA 1986, ss 69(5), 72(3)*].

(c) Instruments first executed outside the UK are stampable as in (a) or (b) above as appropriate, except that the time allowed is 30 days from being received in the UK. [*SA, s 15(3)(a)*].

(d) The Commissioners have a discretion to mitigate or remit any penalty payable on stamping. [*SA, s 15(3)(b)*].

In The Law Society's Gazette of 29 May 1991 the following letter from the Stamp Office was published:

'In recent years, the Board of Inland Revenue has been giving wider publicity to its compliance strategy. One aspect of the strategy is concerned with ensuring that tax and duty are paid at the proper time. It might be helpful to see how this translates into the area of stamp duty with particular reference to those documents presented late for stamping and for which the provisions of *section 15(2)(c)* of the *Stamp Act 1891* come into effect.

In addition to the duty payable, the price to be paid for late stamping is:

- £10 (*section 15(1)*), plus
- interest at 5% per annum on the duty outstanding where this is more than £10 (*section 15(1)*), plus
- a sum equal to the amount of duty outstanding (*section 15(2)(c)*).

In all but those cases of deliberate withholding of duty, avoidance or extreme delay (over one year late), this could be said to be a disproportionately high price to pay. We would not dissent from this view and our practice will be to invoke the authority provided by *section 15(3)(b)* of the *Stamp Act 1891* and mitigate the penalty. The degree of mitigation will be influenced by the reasons for and length of delay. However the minimum level to which a penalty can be expected to be mitigated will reflect interest rates prevailing during the period of delay.

Our offices are instructed in general to mitigate penalties to a level equivalent to an interest rate charge of 12% to 15% per annum for a delay of up to three months, 15% to 20% per annum for three to six months delay, and 20% to 25% for six to twelve months.

Keith Hodgson, Stamp Office, Inland Revenue.'

A further note in The Law Society's Gazette of 9 June 1993 stated:

'*Instruments presented late for stamping*

In the Gazette of 29 May 1991, a letter from the Controller of Stamps, Keith Hodgson, was published, which gave details of the scale of charges which the Stamp Office would apply where instruments were not presented for stamping at the proper time. Since then, there has been a reduction in the level of interest charged, to reflect the general reduction in interest rates, and Stamp Offices are now instructed to mitigate penalties to a level equivalent to an interest rate charge of around 10% per annum for delays of up to three months, and 10% to 15% for three to twelve months'.

63.2 Payment of Duty or Tax

63.2 LIABILITY FOR DUTY AND PENALTIES

See generally 64 PENALTIES AND OFFENCES.

The legislation does not lay down general rules for the liability for duty and penalties. In some cases there is a power of recovery of duty and penalties from persons connected with, but not parties to, the transaction charged. In most cases the duty and penalties are recoverable only when the instrument is produced for stamping. In certain instances, however, the legislation provides for recovery as a debt due to the Crown. These are indicated at 63.3 below. The provision in *SA, s 59(1)* requiring the duty to be paid by the purchaser is not regarded as placing an enforceable obligation on the purchaser to pay the duty.

63.3 The following paragraphs set out the specific rules which apply to the payment of certain stamp duties and penalties.

(*a*) BEARER INSTRUMENTS (13)

   (i) Chargeable on issue—liability for duty, interest and penalties is on the person making the issue or his agent. [*FA 1963, s 60(4)*].

   (ii) Chargeable on transfer—liability for duty, interest and penalties is on the person making the transfer or a broker or agent concerned in the transfer. [*FA 1963, s 60(6)*].

(*b*) BONDS (16). The obligee or covenantee is liable for any penalty for late stamping. [*SA, s 15(2)(d)*].

(*c*) CLEARANCE SERVICES (22). The transferee is liable for any penalty for late stamping. [*FA 1986, s 69(5)*].

(*d*) COMPULSORY PURCHASE (24). The person in whom property is vested or who is authorised to purchase property must produce a duly-stamped document to the Commissioners and in default is liable for duty and interest recoverable as a debt due to the Crown. [*FA 1895, s 12*].

(*e*) CONVEYANCE OR TRANSFER (28) on sale. The transferee or purchaser is liable for any penalty for late stamping. [*SA, s 15(2)(d)*].

(*f*) DEPOSITARY RECEIPTS (34). The transferee is liable for any penalty for late stamping. [*FA 1986, s 72(3)*].

(*g*) LEASES (53). The lessee is liable for any penalty for late stamping. [*SA, s 15(2)*].

(*h*) AGREEMENT FOR LEASE (5). The person contracting for the lease or tack to be granted to him or another is liable for any penalty for late stamping. [*SA, s 15(2)*].

63.4 In addition to the above provisions, any person who receives money in respect of duty but does not apply the money to payment of duty and improperly withholds or detains it is accountable for the duty which is a debt due to the Crown. [*SDMA, s 2*]. This section has been held to apply to a solicitor who withheld from a client a sum for duty (*Lord Advocate v Gordon 1901, 8 SLT 439*).

63.5 ALLOWANCE FOR SPOILED STAMPS

[*SDMA, ss 9–11; Revenue Act 1898, s 13*]

Allowances may be made for spoiled stamps if an application is made within two years after the stamp is spoiled, or, in the case of an executed instrument, the date of the instrument or, if undated, the date of first or only execution. These allowances apply in the following cases.

(*a*) A stamp on any material inadvertently obliterated before the material is signed or the instrument is executed by any party.

(*b*) An adhesive stamp inadvertently spoiled and not affixed to any material.

(*c*) An adhesive stamp representing a fee capable of being collected by such a stamp and which has been affixed to material.

(*d*) A stamp which has been used on any instrument which

(i) is later found to be void from the beginning;

(ii) is later found to be unfit for the original purpose by reason of any error or mistake therein;

(iii) is not used at all and is incomplete or insufficient because of non-signature or non-completion by some party;

(iv) fails the intended purpose or becomes void due to refusal by some person to act thereunder or want of enrolment within a time required by law;

(v) is inadvertently spoiled where another instrument for the same purpose is executed and duly stamped;

(vi) becomes useless because the intended transaction was in fact effected by some other duly stamped instrument.

Allowance may also be made if a stamp of a higher value than necessary has been used inadvertently or if a stamp has been used inadvertently on an instrument not liable to duty.

In the case of an executed instrument, the instrument must be handed in for cancellation but allowance cannot be given if any legal proceeding has commenced where the instrument could be used in evidence.

The allowance is made by giving new stamps to the applicant or by way of refund. See 40 EXTRA-STATUTORY CONCESSIONS for treatment of lost or spoilt documents.

63.6 REPAYMENT FOR UNUSED STAMPS

A person who has a stamp for which he has no use may obtain repayment (after deducting discount) of the stamp provided it is handed in for cancellation within two years of purchase and provided it was purchased from the Inland Revenue or an authorised dealer with a bona fide intention to use it. [*SDMA, s 12*].

63.7 REPAYMENT OF DUTY IN OTHER CASES

(*a*) **Agreements charged as conveyances on sale.** Certain agreements and contracts for sale are chargeable as actual conveyances on sale under *SA, s 59*. (See 6 AGREEMENT FOR SALE.)

Ad valorem duty paid on an agreement is refunded if it is rescinded or annulled or for any reason not substantially performed or carried into effect so as to operate or be followed by a conveyance or transfer. [*SA, s 59(6)*].

(*b*) **Conveyance in contemplation of sale.** Certain conveyances in contemplation of sale are liable to duty as a conveyance or transfer on the value of the property. (See 28.11 CONVEYANCE OR TRANSFER.)

If a claim is made within two years of the conveyance or transfer on the grounds that

(i) the contemplated sale did not take place and the property has been reconveyed to the transferor, or

(ii) the sale took place at a consideration less than the value on which duty was paid,

the excess duty is repaid. [*FA 1965, s 90(2)*].

63.8 CHANGES IN RATES OF DUTY

Changes in rates of duty could formerly be implemented only when a Finance Act received Royal Assent. *FA 1973, s 50* (as amended by *FA 1993 s 207*) gives power to vary or abolish stamp duties by House of Commons resolution for limited periods pending enactment. The resolution has statutory effect from the date stated in the resolution; the date of cessation must also be stated but cannot end later than up to 31 days from the earliest of the following:

(*a*) the 30th day on which the House of Commons sits after the passing of the resolution without a Bill containing the resolution provisions being read a second time and without a Bill being amended to include the provisions;

(*b*) the rejection of a Bill containing the provisions;

(*c*) the dissolution or prorogation of Parliament;

(*d*) the expiration of six months from the day on which the resolution takes effect.

A resolution also ceases to have effect when the Act varying or abolishing the stamp duty comes into effect.

Instruments stamped in accordance with a resolution which has statutory effect under *Sec 50* are validly stamped notwithstanding that the provisions are not ultimately enacted.

For an example of this see *FA 1986, s 78(1)* which reproduces the effect of a 1986 Budget resolution withdrawing the exemption for transfers of loan capital. The resolution was subsequently withdrawn by the Government and the exemption reinstated so a statutory provision was enacted to give effect to the withdrawal of the exemption for the period from 25 March 1986 to 6 July 1986 during which time a charge on transfers of loan capital therefore arose.

63.9 STAMP DUTY RESERVE TAX

See 73.6 STAMP DUTY RESERVE TAX and 3.8 ADMINISTRATION.

---

64   Penalties and Offences

64.1 The majority of the penalties and offences are specific to a head of charge or type of instrument, but reference should be made to 64.8 below which deals with penalties and offences applicable to stamp duties generally.

64.2 FINES AND PENALTIES

The distinction between fines and penalties (which are indicated in the following paragraphs) imposed for various offences is generally as follows.

Fines—recoverable by High Court proceedings.

Penalties—must be paid on stamping of the instrument, the sanction being refusal by the Commissioners to stamp.

Heading and Offence	*Fine or Penalty*	*Legislation*

64.3 BEARER INSTRUMENTS (13)

(*a*) Chargeable on issue—non-compliance with *FA 1963, s 60(3)(13.5(a))*.	Maximum fine £50 plus amount equal to duty. Also the duty due with interest at 5% p.a. from the date of default.	*FA 1963, s 60(4)*
(*b*) Chargeable on transfer—transfer by instrument not duly stamped.	As above.	*FA 1963, s 60(6)*
(*c*) Furnishing false particulars of instruments wilfully or negligently.	Maximum fine £50 plus twice difference between duty actually paid and duty chargeable.	*FA 1963, s 60(7)*

64.4   Penalties and Offences

Heading and Offence	Fine or Penalty	Legislation
64.4 CLEARANCE SERVICES (22)		
Failure to notify Commissioners of relevant facts.	Maximum fines £1,000 or £100.	*FA 1986, s 71(2)–(5)*
64.5 COMPULSORY PURCHASE (24)		
Non-production of Act or vesting instrument.	Interest on duty of 5% p.a. from date of Act or vesting.	*FA 1895, s 12*
64.6 DEPOSITARY RECEIPTS (34)		
Failure to notify Commissioners of relevant facts.	Maximum fines £1,000 or £100.	*FA 1986, s 68(1)(2)(4)(5)*
64.7 INSTRUMENTS (49)		
Not setting out facts fully and truly with intent to defraud.	Maximum fine £25	*SA, s 5*
64.8 PAYMENT OF DUTY OR TAX (62)		
(*a*) Stamping after execution.	Maximum penalty £10 plus interest at 5% p.a. up to amount of duty.	*SA, s 15(1)*
(*b*) Delay, non-stamping or insufficient stamping without reasonable excuse of certain instruments (see 63 PAYMENT OF DUTY OR TAX) with ad valorem duty.	Maximum fine £10 plus penalty as in (*a*) plus penalty equal to duty.	*SA, s 15(2)(c)*
64.9 PRODUCED STAMPS (65)		
Failure to produce instrument or comply with *FA 1931, 2 Sch.*	Maximum fine £50	*FA 1931, s 28(1); Land Commission Act 1967, s 87, 14 Sch*
64.10 SHARES AND SECURITIES (71)		
(*a*) Transfer etc. of foreign or Commonwealth government security not duly stamped.	Maximum fine £20	*SA, s 83; FA 1963, s 62(4); FA 1973, 22 Sch*

Heading and Offence	*Fine or Penalty*	*Legislation*
(*b*) Blank transfers. Parting with possession or removing from GB a blank transfer not duly completed.	Maximum fine £50 plus twice duty chargeable on original transfer in blank.	*FA 1963, s 67(1)*

64.11 OFFENCES RELATING TO STAMPS

(*a*) Dealers in stamps.

(i) Unauthorised dealing.	Maximum fine £50	*SDMA, s 4(1) as amended by Criminal Law Act 1977, s 31(5)(6)*
(ii) Advertisement of dealing.	Maximum fine £25	*SDMA, s 4(2) as amended as above*
(*b*) Fraudulent acts in connection with stamps.	Maximum sentence six months' imprisonment on summary conviction; 14 years on indictment	*SDMA, s 13; Forgery Act 1913*
(*c*) Fraud generally.	Maximum fine £50	*SDMA, s 21*
(*d*) Adhesive stamps.		
(i) Defacement.	Maximum fine £25	*SDMA, s 20 as amended by CLA 1977, s 31(5)(6)*
(ii) Fraudulent removal and re-use or sale.	Maximum fine £50 plus 'any other fine or penalty to which he may be liable'	*SA, s 9*

64.12 MISCELLANEOUS

(*a*) Refusal by public officer to permit inspection of rolls, books etc. by Commissioners.	Maximum fine £10	*SA, s 16*
(*b*) Registration of an instrument not duly stamped.	Maximum fine £10	*SA, s 17*

65 Powers of Attorney

65.1 The head of charge 'Letters or Powers of Attorney etc.' was abolished by *FA 1985, s 85, 24 Sch (g)*.

66 Produced Stamp

[FA 1931, s 28, 2 Sch; Land Commission Act 1967, s 87, 14 Sch]

66.1 The following instruments must be produced to the Commissioners:

(*a*) the transfer on sale of fee simple of land;

(*b*) the grant or lease of land for a term of seven years or more;

(*c*) transfer on sale of a lease as in (*b*).

An AGREEMENT FOR LEASE (5) for a term of more than seven years must also be produced but a lease granted in pursuance of the agreement and consistent with it need not be produced.

66.2 Production must be made within 30 days of execution (or 30 days from being received in GB if executed abroad) and the obligation to produce is on the transferee or lessee.

66.3 The Commissioners will stamp the instrument with a stamp denoting that it has been produced. The produced stamp is required in addition to any stamp denoting duty and any adjudication stamp; the instrument is not duly stamped unless it bears a produced stamp.

66.4 The particulars required to be given to the Commissioners in respect of a produced instrument are found in *FA 1931, 2 Sch* as amended and are set out in the 'Particulars Delivered' form (form L(A) 451) used for this purpose.

66.5 An instrument relating solely to incorporeal heriditaments or a grave or right of burial need not be produced.

66.6 The purpose of these requirements is to give district valuers information on land values.

66.7 Since 1 January 1986 a new procedure has applied in relation to transfers of registered freehold or leasehold land which contain a CERTIFICATE OF VALUE (19) i.e. on which no stamp duty is payable. The new procedure does not apply to the grant of a lease or to transfers which require ADJUDICATION (2).

Where it applies, the new procedure requires the 'Particulars Delivered' form to be sent direct to the appropriate District Land Registry (together with the transfer and application for registration), and not to the Stamp Office. [*FA 1985, s 89; The Stamp Duty (Exempt Instruments) Regulations 1985 (SI 1985 No 1688)*].

---

67   Purchase of Own Shares

67.1   When a company purchases its own shares under *Companies Act 1985, s 162*, the shares can be delivered to the company and surrendered by the shareholder without the need for an instrument of transfer. However, under *Companies Act 1985, s 169* the company is required to file a return providing details of the purchase with the Registrar of Companies within 28 days of the shares being delivered to the company. This return is deemed to be an instrument transferring the shares on sale to the company and is accordingly chargeable with ad valorem duty under the head CONVEYANCE OR TRANSFER (28) on sale at the rate of 50p per £100 or part of £100. [*FA 1986, s 66*].

67.2   No duty arises on the redemption of redeemable shares under *Companies Act 1985, s 160*. In appropriate cases exemption under *FA 1930, s 42* is available. (See 12 ASSOCIATED COMPANIES.)

---

68   Receipts

68.1   The former head of charge applying to receipts in *SA, 1 Sch* was abolished by *FA 1970, 8 Sch*.

Duty may be charged under some other head. An acknowledgement of receipt of the purchase price of a reversionary interest was held to be liable to ad valorem duty as an AGREEMENT FOR SALE (6) or as a CONVEYANCE OR TRANSFER (28) on sale of an equitable interest (*Fleetwood-Hesketh v CIR CA, [1936] 1 KB 351*).

69 Release and Renunciation

69.1 A release or renunciation of any property or right or interest in property is charged to duty as follows:

(*a*) on a sale—ad valorem duty as a conveyance on sale (see 28 CONVEYANCE OR TRANSFER);

(*b*) any other case—fixed duty of 50p.

[*SA, 1 Sch*].

69.2 For a release or renunciation to be chargeable it must relate to property and amount to a transfer or assignment. The following have been held, inter alia, not to be chargeable as releases:

(*a*) an undertaking not to work coal (*Great Northern Railway v CIR CA, [1901] 1 KB 416*);

(*b*) a release of a widow's claim to *jus relictae* under Scottish law (*Cormack's Trustees v CIR CS, 1924 SC 819*).

69.3 **Disclaimers.** A release or renunciation entails acquisition of proprietary rights and subsequent disposition. A disclaimer on the other hand operates as a refusal to accept proprietary rights and cannot therefore be charged under the head Release etc. or as a CONVEYANCE OR TRANSFER (28) on sale. (*Re Stratton's Deed of Disclaimer CA 1957, [1958] Ch 42; Re Paradise Motor Co CA, [1968] 2 All ER 625*).

69.4 Renounceable letters of allotment and acceptance are not chargeable under this head. These documents will normally attract STAMP DUTY RESERVE TAX (73) on sale.

70 Scotland

70.1 The stamp duty legislation in this book applies to Scotland but its application requires some adaption to Scottish law. There are also a few heads of charge dealt with in the following paragraphs which relate only to instruments which have effect under Scottish law.

Head of charge	Duty	Legislation
70.2 **Bond** on obtaining confirmation of testament.	Exempt	*FA 1949, s 35, 8 Sch 8*
70.3 **Dispositions**		
(*a*) of heritable property to singular successors or purchasers;	See CONVEYANCE OR TRANSFER (28)	*SA, 1 Sch*
(*b*) of heritable property to a purchaser containing a clause declaring the purchase money a real burden on or affecting that property;	See CONVEYANCE OR TRANSFER (28)	*SA, 1 Sch*
(*c*) containing constitution of feu or ground annual right;	See CONVEYANCE OR TRANSFER (28)	*SA, 1 Sch*
(*d*) of any property or right or interest therein not elsewhere described.	50p	*SA, 1 Sch*
70.4 Tack of lands etc.	See LEASES (53)	*SA, 1 Sch*

70.5 **PRODUCED STAMP (66)**

Since 1 September 1974 the grant or transfer on sale of a lease of land in Scotland does not need to be produced to the Commissioners under *FA 1931, s 28* if the term of the lease exceeds 20 years. [*Land Tenure Reform (Scotland) Act 1974*].

71   Scrip Dividends

71.1 A scrip dividend is a dividend in the form of additional shares rather than in cash. The shares are allotted fully paid-up out of the company's distributable reserves. No stamp duty arises on the making of a scrip dividend. The old head of charge 'Scrip Certificate, Scrip or other document' was abolished by *FA 1949, s 35, 8 Sch.*

72 Shares and Securities

Note. The stamp duty and stamp duty reserve tax charges in relation to shares and securities were to be abolished from a date to be appointed by statutory instrument. [*FA 1990, ss 108–111*]. But see 1.1 INTRODUCTION.

See also STAMP DUTY RESERVE TAX (73).

72.1 The following paragraphs summarise the stamp duty implications of transactions in shares and securities

(*a*) on issue (72.2–72.3);

(*b*) on transfer—generally (72.4–72.8);

(*c*) on transfer to market makers etc. (72.9);

(*d*) on transfer in connection with DEPOSITARY RECEIPTS (34) or CLEARANCE SERVICES (22) (72.10);

(*e*) special categories of stock (72.11).

Where an agreement to transfer shares or securities is not followed by a duly stamped instrument transferring the shares or securities to the purchaser within two months of the agreement a charge to STAMP DUTY RESERVE TAX (73) will normally arise. The tax will be refunded, or if not paid the charge will be cancelled, if a duly stamped transfer is subsequently created within six years of the agreement.

An important exception to this is LETTERS OF ALLOTMENT AND ACCEPTANCE (54) renounceable within six months. Because these letters are exempt from stamp duty a STAMP DUTY RESERVE TAX (73) charge arises automatically on each sale of a letter within the renunciation period.

72.2 ISSUE OF SHARES

FA 1988, s 141 abolished the CAPITAL DUTY (18) chargeable on the issue of shares by a capital company. Shares may be issued as the consideration for a sale and therefore ad valorem duty under the head CONVEYANCE OR TRANSFER (28) on sale may be payable on the transfer of the property sold calculated according to the value of the shares issued. But see the exemptions and relief from stamp duty for COMPANY REORGANISATIONS (23). The issue of bearer shares may attract duty under the head BEARER INSTRUMENTS (13).

72.3 ISSUE OF OTHER SECURITIES

Since the abolition of the heads 'Marketable Security' and 'Loan Capital' [*FA 1973, 22 Sch*], duty is not generally charged on the issue of securities other than shares. Certain bearer securities are, however, chargeable on issue.

72.4 TRANSFERS OF SHARES GENERALLY

(a) **On sale.** The sale of shares etc. is liable to duty as a CONVEYANCE OR TRANSFER (28) on sale. The reduced rates of ad valorem duty applicable to certified instruments do not apply, as a CERTIFICATE OF VALUE (19) cannot be given in respect of transfers of stocks, shares, and marketable securities. A limited number of bearer instruments are chargeable on transfer and a transfer on sale will be liable under the head BEARER INSTRUMENTS (13). There is currently available a scheme which appears to have been successful in avoiding ad valorem stamp duty on the sale of shares in UK companies. The scheme relies on the exemptions from stamp duty and STAMP DUTY RESERVE TAX (73) for bearer instruments expressed in a foreign currency. See 13.7(a) BEARER INSTRUMENTS and 73.5(b) STAMP DUTY RESERVE TAX. The scheme involves the following steps:

(i) the existing ordinary shares of the target company are converted into deferred shares worth very little and share warrants to bearer denominated in a foreign currency are issued to the shareholders of the target by way of bonus issue capitalised from the target's reserves;

(ii) the share warrants to bearer are sold by delivery for most of the agreed sale price of the target and the deferred shares are transferred for the balance of the sale price in the normal way with stamp duty being paid only in respect of the latter transfer.

Several detailed company law and capital gains tax points need to be considered by the vendor when using this scheme and it may be appropriate to seek an indemnity from the purchaser for the risks and costs involved.

(b) **By gift.** A transfer of shares etc. by way of gift no longer attracts ad valorem duty following the abolition of the charge on GIFTS (47) by *FA 1985, s 82*. However, even if the transfer is not a sale at undervalue it will still be necessary to submit it for ADJUDICATION (2) and pay a fixed duty of 50p under the head 'CONVEYANCE OR TRANSFER (28) of any kind not hereinbefore described' unless the transfer is certified in accordance with *The Stamp Duty (Exempt Instruments) Regulations 1987 (SI 1987 No 516)*. See 39 EXEMPT INSTRUMENTS.

(c) **By exchange.** A transaction of exchange involving shares is not liable under the head EXCHANGE OR PARTITION (37) (*Coates (J & P) Ltd v CIR CA, [1897] 2 QB 423*), but is liable to ad valorem duty as a CONVEYANCE OR TRANSFER (28) on sale (although see 23 COMPANY REORGANISATIONS for relief from duty).

72.5 Subject to regulations to be made under *Companies Act 1989, s 207*, it is unlawful for a company to register a transfer of shares in the company or debentures of the company unless a proper instrument of transfer has been delivered to it (unless the transfer arises by operation of law). [*Companies Act 1985, s 183(1)(2)*]. A registrar who registers a transfer of shares or debentures which has not been duly stamped is liable to a fine of £10. [*SA, s 17*]. *Companies Act 1989, s 207* provides for regulations to be made to enable title to securities to be evidenced and transferred without a written instrument.

72.6 The *Stock Transfer Act 1963*, as amended, provides for standard forms to be used for the transfer of the registered securities of

(i)   companies limited by shares;

(ii) certain other bodies incorporated in Great Britain;

(iii) the Government, other than Post Office securities and national savings certificates;

(iv) local authorities;

(v)   unit trusts.

72.7 **Blank transfers** may be used to effect the transfer by sale of registered stock. A transfer in blank is one where the name of the transferee has not been inserted. It is an offence (see 64 PENALTIES AND OFFENCES) to part with possession of the blank transfer or remove it from Great Britain before it is duly completed (which means the insertion of the names of the purchaser, his agent or nominee or a person entitled to a charge on the stock for money lent to the purchaser or donee). [*FA 1963, s 67*]. The purpose of this provision is to ensure that duty is charged on transfers on sale of registered stock.

72.8 **Stock Exchange transactions.** In order to enable the implementation of The Stock Exchange's computerised transfer and settlement system ('Talisman'), special rules were introduced by *FA 1976, s 127* concerning transfers involving stock exchange nominees (persons designated for the purposes of *FA 1976, s 127* by the Secretary of State). Under *Sec 127* transfers to the nominee company of The International Stock Exchange, SEPON Ltd, executed for the purposes of a stock exchange transaction are exempt from duty.

72.9 **TRANSFERS OF SHARES TO MARKET MAKERS ETC.**

There are two exemptions from stamp duty available only to market makers. Where either exemption applies no stamp duty is charged on a transfer of shares or securities to the market maker (or his nominee) acting in the ordinary course of his business as a market maker in shares or securities of the kind transferred. However, the transfer must be stamped with a DENOT-ING STAMP to indicate that no stamp duty is chargeable. [*FA 1986, s 81(1)(2)*].

The first and wider exemption is available to dealers who are members of The International Stock Exchange and who are registered market makers. Transfers of shares and securities to such persons are exempt from stamp duty provided the transfer is in the ordinary course of that person's business as a market maker in shares or securities of the kind transferred. The exemption is available whether the shares or securities transferred are listed on The International Stock Exchange, or dealt in on the Unlisted Securities Market or are of off-market shares or securities. [*FA 1986, s 81(3)(a); FA 1986 (Stamp Duty and Stamp Duty Reserve Tax) (Amendment) Regulations 1988 (SI 1988 No 654)*].

A second and narrower exemption is available to dealers who are not members of The International Stock Exchange. This exemption is available only for transfers to the dealer of off-market shares or securities i.e. shares and securities that are not listed on The International Stock Exchange or dealt in on the Unlisted Securities Market. The dealer will qualify for this exemption if

(*a*) he is authorised to carry out investment business under the *FSA 1986*;

(*b*) he carried out the transaction in the course of his business as a dealer in investments as a principal; and

(*c*) he did not carry out the transaction in the course of managing investments or in connection with a collective investment scheme.

[*FA 1986, s 81(3)(b); FA 1986 (Stamp Duty and Stamp Duty Reserve Tax) (Amendment) Regulations 1988 (SI 1988 No 654)*]. (See also 73.3 STAMP DUTY RESERVE TAX.)

A maximum duty of 50p is charged on transfers of shares and securities in connection with stock lending arrangements. [*FA 1986, s 82*].

72.10 **TRANSFERS IN CONNECTION WITH DEPOSITARY RECEIPTS (34) AND CLEARANCE SERVICES (22)**

A special charge arises on transfers of certain shares and securities in connection with such schemes. See the chapters referred to above.

72.11 **SPECIAL CATEGORIES OF STOCK**

(*a*) Government stocks are exempt from all stamp duties. [*SA, 1 Sch*].

(*b*) Treasury guaranteed stocks are transferable free of all stamp duties. [*FA 1947, s 57*].

(*c*) No stamp duty is charged on the issue or transfer of the stock of a designated international organisation. [*FA 1984, s 126*].

(*d*) LOAN CAPITAL AND DEBENTURES (55). Most forms of loan capital and debenture are now exempt from all stamp duties.

(*e*) Warrants to purchase Government stock are themselves exempt from all stamp duties. [*FA 1987, s 50; F(No 2)A 1987, s 99*]. See 59 OPTIONS AND EQUITY WARRANTS.

(*f*) Paired shares. Units comprising paired shares of the type issued by Eurotunnel are treated as single shares for both stamp duty and STAMP DUTY RESERVE TAX (73). [*FA 1988, ss 143, 144*].

73 Stamp Duty Reserve Tax

Note. Stamp duty reserve tax was to be abolished from a date to be appointed by statutory instrument. [*FA 1990, ss 110, 111*]. But see 1.1 INTRODUCTION.

73.1 GENERAL

A chain of agreements for the sale of shares or securities followed by an instrument of transfer from the first seller direct to the last purchaser normally results in stamp duty being charged only once on the instrument of transfer according to the price paid by the last purchaser. All the intermediate sale agreements escape stamp duty. This is because agreements for the sale of a legal interest in stock or marketable securities escape stamp duty under *SA, s 59(1)* (see 6.3 AGREEMENT FOR SALE) and the instrument of transfer is only charged with duty in respect of the price paid by the last purchaser under *SA, s 58(4)* (see 6.12 AGREEMENT FOR SALE). This meant that it was possible to deal in shares or securities during a Stock Exchange period of account without paying stamp duty. Only the transfer to the ultimate purchaser at the end of the account would attract stamp duty.

Stamp duty reserve tax was introduced to impose an ad valorem charge on the intermediate sale agreements. The tax is charged at the same rate as stamp duty on a CONVEYANCE OR TRANSFER (28) on sale i.e. at 50p per £100 of the price paid. Unlike stamp duty, the tax applies to the agreement to transfer (whether oral or written) and does not depend upon the execution of a written instrument of transfer for a charge to arise. However, if an instrument transferring the shares or securities to the purchaser is executed and duly stamped within two months of the agreement to transfer, no tax charge can arise.

Stamp duty reserve tax is not a stamp duty but a separate tax with its own rules, procedure and collection machinery. It applies to agreements to transfer *chargeable securities* for consideration in money or money's worth and hence is wider in scope than conveyance on sale duty which arises only when the consideration is money, shares or securities and debts. However, when the consideration is not money, shares or securities or debts there will not normally be a sale for stamp duty purposes and the share transfer will attract only a fixed 50p stamp which will prevent a stamp duty reserve tax charge arising. Although most of the exemptions and reliefs from stamp duty have no equivalents in stamp duty reserve tax, a share transfer which is submitted for ADJUDICATION (2) and stamped exempt from stamp duty counts as a duly stamped instrument and as such prevents any stamp duty reserve tax charge arising.

There are three types of stamp duty reserve tax charge: the principal charge (see 73.2–73.6 below) and the charges in relation to CLEARANCE SERVICES (22) and DEPOSITARY RECEIPTS (34).

73.2 THE PRINCIPAL CHARGE [*FA 1986, s 87*]

The principal charge applies where a person (A) agrees with another person (B) to transfer *chargeable securities* for consideration in money or money's worth unless an instrument transferring the securities to B or his nominee is executed and duly stamped within two months of the agreement. The charge is at the rate of 50p per £100 or part of £100 of the amount or value of the consideration. The open market value of the consideration is taken when the consideration is not money. When B agrees to buy chargeable securities from A and resells some of those securities to C the tax has effect as if there were two separate agreements between A and B. The first agreement relates to the securities which B retains and in respect of which an instrument transferring the securities to him is executed and stamped within two months. No stamp duty reserve tax arises on this agreement. The second agreement between A and B relates to the securities which B has resold to C and in respect of which there will be a duly stamped instrument transferring the securities direct from A to C. Stamp duty reserve tax is charged on this second agreement between A and B according to the price paid by B because there will be no instrument transferring those securities to B. The following example illustrates this:

B buys 10,000 shares from A for £10,000
B resells 7,500 of the shares to C
A transfers 2,500 shares to B and 7,500 shares direct to C

B is treated as if he had made two agreements. The first relates to the 2,500 shares transferred to him by A on which B will pay stamp duty on £2,500. The second agreement relates to the 7,500 shares which B has sub-sold to C and on which B will pay stamp duty reserve tax on £7,500. C will pay stamp duty on the transfer of the 7,500 shares direct from A. Where *chargeable securities* are transferred not to B but to a bank or other person as security for a loan made to B, the lender is treated as if he were B's nominee. Therefore, a duly stamped instrument transferring the securities to the lender instead of B will nevertheless forestall a stamp duty reserve tax charge.

The stamp duty reserve tax legislation fails to identify clearly who A and B are when buyer and/or seller act through agents, as for example when an investor buys securities on The International Stock Exchange through a broker. In their revised edition of 'Stamp Duty Reserve Tax—Notes for guidance' published in June 1993 the Stamp Office state:

'7.3. . . . . Where securities are bought on The Stock Exchange via a broker acting as agent, the buying broker will normally be the person responsible for accounting for it to the Inland Revenue though his client will be liable. The contractual arrangement between the broker and his client does not constitute a *separate* chargeable agreement. Where an investor buys securities direct from a Stock Exchange member firm (i.e. where the firm is selling as a principal) the person ultimately liable in law for the tax will be the investor; but under the *Regulations* the Stock Exchange firm will be responsible for notifying the Revenue of the charge and accounting for the tax.'

73.2   Stamp Duty Reserve Tax

The 1993 edition of the Notes reflects a change of view by the Stamp Office from the previous October 1986 edition in which it was clear that in Stock Exchange transactions the Stamp Office were treating the agents and not their client principals as A and B. One problem with this old approach was that there would be no duly stamped instrument transferring the securities to the person treated as B i.e. the buying broker-dealer. The transfer would of course be direct to the client principal and could not therefore forestall a stamp duty reserve tax charge on the broker-dealer. A double charge should therefore arise consisting of stamp duty reserve tax on the broker-dealer and stamp duty on the client principal. To avoid this the Stamp Office also stated in their 'Notes for guidance':

'2.4   To allow time for an instrument of transfer to be produced *Section 87* provides for the charge to arise two months after the date of the agreement, unless in the meantime a duly stamped instrument of transfer has been executed (normally this would be a stock transfer form or, in the case of most Stock Exchange transactions, a TALIS-MAN bought transfer) transferring the securities either to the person described in paragraph 2.1 above as B or B's nominee. Where in the case of a transaction carried out on The Stock Exchange the agreement is concluded between a member firm selling as a principal and a broker-dealer acting as an agent, this condition is regarded as satisfied if within the two-month period a duly stamped instrument of transfer is executed transferring the securities to which the agreement relates to the broker-dealer's principal.'

The old approach by the Stamp Office seemed to be limited to Stock Exchange transactions and they did not seek to make agents liable in other situations e.g. offers for sale and placings where the sponsoring bank acts not as purchaser and seller but as 'agent to procure' purchasers to avoid a charge to stamp duty reserve tax on the sponsor. However, the Stamp Office have now changed their view as to who A and B are. Evidence for this first appeared in the amendments made to the definition of 'accountable person' in *The Stamp Duty Reserve Tax Regulations 1986 (SI 1986 No 1711)* by *The Stamp Duty Reserve Tax (Amendment) Regulations 1988 (SI 1988 No 835)* (see 73.6 below). The relevant part of the amended definition now reads:

'"*accountable person*" means

(*a*) in relation to a charge under *section 87* of the Act ("*section 87*")

(i) if the person mentioned as B in *section 87(1)* is a market maker or broker and dealer, or if a broker and dealer is acting as an agent for B who is not a market maker or broker and dealer, the market maker or broker and dealer, and failing that

(ii) if the person mentioned as A in *section 87(1)* is a market maker or broker and dealer, or if a broker and dealer is acting as an agent for B who is not a market maker or broker and dealer, the market maker or broker and dealer, ...'

It is clear from the amended *Regulations* that in relation to Stock Exchange transactions the client principals are A and B and not their agents. A and B are therefore the principals and not their agents in all transactions regardless of whether a transaction is on The International Stock Exchange or not. The 1993 'Notes for guidance' now confirm this.

Renounceable letters of allotment and acceptance are *chargeable securities* and dealings in renounceable letters where the rights under the letter are renounceable not later than six months after the issue of the letter attract stamp duty reserve tax. The tax charge arises automatically on the date of each agreement to transfer a renounceable letter. There is no two-month waiting period to allow time for a duly stamped instrument of transfer to be created because letters of allotment etc. where the rights are renounceable not later than six months after issue are exempt from stamp duty. [*FA 1986, ss 88(2)(3), 90(3)*]. See 54 LETTERS OF ALLOTMENT AND ACCEPTANCE, 44 FLOTATIONS, ETC. and 13 BEARER INSTRUMENTS.

Stamp duty reserve tax is the liability of the purchaser, i.e. the person referred to as B above. [*FA 1986, s 91; F(No 2)A 1987, s 100(2)*]. Where a tax charge has arisen and within six years of the date of the agreement an instrument transferring the chargeable securities to B or his nominee is executed and duly stamped, the tax, if paid, is repayable, and if not paid, is no longer payable. Repayments of £25 or more carry tax-free interest from the date the tax was paid until the repayment order is issued. The interest is calculated at the rate applicable under *FA 1989, s 178*. [*FA 1986, s 92* and *FA 1989, ss 179, 180*].

73.3 MARKET MAKERS

There are three exemptions from stamp duty reserve tax available to market makers. Where an exemption applies no stamp duty reserve tax is charged on the transfer of shares or securities to the market maker (or his nominee) in the ordinary course of his business as a dealer in shares or securities of the kind transferred.

The first and widest exemption is available to market makers who are members of The International Stock Exchange and who are registered as market makers. Transfers of shares and securities to such persons are exempt from stamp duty reserve tax provided the transfer is in the ordinary course of that person's business as a market maker in shares or securities of the kind transferred. The exemption is available whether the shares or securities transferred are listed on The International Stock Exchange, dealt in on the Unlisted Securities Market or are off-market shares or securities. [*FA 1986, s 89(1)(3)(a); FA 1986 (Stamp Duty and Stamp Duty Reserve Tax) (Amendment) Regulations 1988 (SI 1988 No 654)*].

The second and narrower exemption is available to dealers who are not members of The International Stock Exchange. This exemption is available only for transfers to the dealer of off-market shares or securities i.e. shares and securities that are not listed on The International Stock

73.4 Stamp Duty Reserve Tax

Exchange or dealt in on the Unlisted Securities Market. The dealer will qualify for this exemption if

(*a*) he is authorised to carry out investment business under the *FSA 1986*;

(*b*) he makes the agreement in the course of his business as a dealer in investments as a principal; and

(*c*) he did not make the agreement in the course of managing investments or in connection with a collective investment scheme. [*FA 1986, s 89(2)(3)(b); FA 1986 (Stamp Duty and Stamp Duty Reserve Tax) (Amendment) Regulations 1988 (SI 1988 No 654)*].

The third exemption is available for transfers of related quoted options to market makers in such securities. [*FA 1986, s 89(1A)*]. (See also 72.9 SHARES AND SECURITIES.)

73.4 BROKER-DEALERS

Stamp duty reserve tax is not charged on the transfer of securities to a person if

(*a*) that person buys as principal in the ordinary course of his business as a broker-dealer in securities of that kind, and

(*b*) he sells the securities before the end of the period of seven days beginning with the day he bought them.

A person is a broker-dealer if he is a member of The International Stock Exchange, carries on business in the UK and is not a market maker in securities of that kind.

There are rules for identifying sales with purchases where this is not otherwise possible:

(i) securities of the same kind acquired in the seven days ending on the day of the sale and not already matched with a sale are taken before securities acquired outside that period;

(ii) securities of the same kind acquired earlier in the seven-day period in (i) are taken before securities acquired later in that period.

[*FA 1986, s 89(2)(4)(7)(8)*].

73.5 OTHER EXEMPTIONS

See 44 FLOTATIONS, ETC. for the exemption for offers of existing and new shares. [*FA 1986, s 89A*].

The following exemptions are also available:

(*a*) certain transfers of units under a unit trust scheme, see 77 UNIT TRUSTS;

(*b*) transfers of overseas bearer instruments, or of inland bearer instruments which do not fall within the stamp duty exemption for renounceable letters of allotment etc. where the rights are renounceable not later

than six months after issue, see 13 BEARER INSTRUMENTS and 54 LETTERS
OF ALLOTMENT AND ACCEPTANCE;

(*c*) transfers which are caught by the special charges in relation to
CLEARANCE SERVICES (22) and DEPOSITARY RECEIPTS (34);

(*d*) transfers where the securities are held by a nominee or agent for the
provider of CLEARANCE SERVICES (22) and the business of the nominee or
agent is exclusively that of holding securities for such a person;

(*e*) transfers of securities to CHARITIES (21) and similar bodies. [*FA 1986,
s 90*].

73.6 LIABILITY AND ACCOUNTABILITY

The person liable to pay stamp duty reserve tax is the purchaser, i.e. the
person referred to as B in 73.2 above. [*FA 1986, s 91; F(No 2)A 1987,
s 100(2)*]. The tax must be paid by the *accountable date* which means the last
day of the month following the month in which the charge arises. The charge
itself will not arise until two months after the date of the agreement.
Therefore if B agrees to buy chargeable securities from A on 9 May 1988 a
charge will arise on 9 July 1988 and the tax must be paid by 31 August 1988.
[*The Stamp Duty Reserve Tax Regulations 1986 (SI 1986 No 1711),
Regs 2, 3*].

In relation to agreements to transfer renounceable letters of allotment or
acceptance the charge arises on the date of the agreement and the tax must
be paid by the last day of the month following the month in which the charge
arises, i.e. there is no two-month waiting period. [*FA 1986, s 88(2)(3); FA
1987, 7 Sch 1, 3*].

The **accountable person** is required under regulations to give notice that a
stamp duty reserve tax charge has arisen and to pay the tax. The definition of
accountable person as originally found in the *Regulations* has been changed
and the effect of this change in relation to the identity of A and B is
considered in 73.2 above. Under the new definition the *accountable person* is

(*a*) the buying *market maker* or *broker-dealer* including a *broker-dealer*
acting as agent for his client who is not a *market maker* or *broker-
dealer* and failing that

(*b*) the selling *market maker* or *broker-dealer* including a *broker-dealer*
acting as agent for his client, who is not a *market maker* or *broker-
dealer* and failing that

(*c*) the buying *qualified dealer* including a dealer acting as agent for his
client who is not a *qualified dealer* and failing that

(*d*) the selling *qualified dealer* including a dealer acting as agent for his client
who is not a *qualified dealer* and failing that

(*e*) B i.e. the purchaser, where no *market maker, broker-dealer* or *qualified
dealer* is involved in the transaction.

Market maker has the same meaning as it has in 73.3 above. **Broker-dealer** has the same meaning as it has in 73.4 above. A **qualified dealer** means a person who, not being a *market maker* or a *broker-dealer*, is authorised to conduct investment business under the *FSA 1986*. The definition of *qualified dealer* has been extended to include a European Institution within the meaning of the *Banking Coordination (Second Council Directive) Regulations 1992 (SI 1992 No 3218)* which came into force on 1 January 1993. These regulations give effect to the *Second Council Directive 89/646* on the coordination of laws, regulations and administrative provisions relating to the taking-up and pursuit of the business of credit institutions under the terms of the *Directive*, credit institutions incorporated in a member State and certain of their subsidiaries which may conduct a wide range of banking and other financial services throughout the EC. This requires the extension of the definition of *qualified dealer* to include such institutions and subsidiaries conducting services in the UK. [*The Stamp Duty Reserve Tax (Amendment) Regulations 1992 (SI 1992 No 3287)*].

The intention is that the collection and payment of the tax is carried out by the market professionals and not individual investors. The Controller of Stamps can authorise different arrangements for the collection and payment of tax and this is normally done in the case of FLOTATIONS, ETC. (44) where the vendor or relevant government minister is designated the *accountable person*. The relevant prospectus will mention this. [*The Stamp Duty Reserve Tax Regulations 1986 (SI 1986 No 1711), Regs 2, 4; The Stamp Duty Reserve Tax (Amendment) Regulations 1988 (SI 1988 No 835)*].

73.7   CHARGEABLE SECURITIES

Chargeable securities are:

(a)   stocks, shares or loan capital,

(b)   interests in, or in dividends or other rights arising out of stocks, shares or loan capital,

(c)   rights to allotments of or to subscribe for, or options to acquire, stocks, shares or loan capital, and

(d)   units under a unit trust scheme.

With the exemption of units under a unit trust scheme, securities issued or raised by a company not incorporated in the UK are not *chargeable securities* unless:

(i)   they are registered in a register kept in the UK by or on behalf of the company, or

(ii)   the shares are paired with shares issued by a company incorporated in the UK, or

(iii)   in the case of securities falling within (b) and (c) above, the underlying securities are registered in a UK register or are paired with shares issued by a company incorporated in the UK.

The reference in (ii) and (iii) above to shares being paired with shares of a

UK incorporated company means that each unit representing paired shares of the type issued by Eurotunnel is treated as a single *chargeable security*.

Securities which are exempt from stamp duty on transfer (e.g. gilts, and securities falling within (*b*) and (*c*) above where the underlying securities are exempt from stamp duty on transfer) are not *chargeable securities*. Also excluded from the meaning of *chargeable securities* are interests in DEPOSITARY RECEIPTS (34) for stocks or shares.

[*FA 1986, s 99(3)–(6a); FA 1988, s 144(1)(2)*].

73.8   In relation to the special charges on DEPOSITARY RECEIPTS (34) and CLEARANCE SERVICES (22) the definition of *chargeable securities* in 73.7 above applies except that (i) is ignored so that securities issued or raised by a company not incorporated in the UK but registered in a register kept in the UK are not *chargeable securities*. In the case of newly-subscribed shares or securities within (*b*) and (*c*) representing such shares, (ii) is ignored so that such securities issued by a company not incorporated in the UK but paired with shares issued by a company incorporated in the UK are not *chargeable securities* when issued in pursuance of arrangements for clearance services or depositary receipts. Also, shares registered in an overseas branch register which are exempt from stamp duty on transfer by *Companies Act 1985, 14 Sch 8* are still *chargeable securities* despite this exemption. [*FA 1986, s 99(10)–(12); FA 1988, s 144(4)(5)*].

73.9   **ADMINISTRATION AND INTEREST ON OVERDUE TAX**

As mentioned above, regulations have been made under *FA 1986, s 98* governing the administration, assessment, collection and recovery of stamp duty reserve tax. These regulations are *The Stamp Duty Reserve Tax Regulations 1986 (SI 1986 No 1711* as amended by *SI 1988 No 835* and *SI 1989 No 1301*) and they also provide for the application of provisions of the *Taxes Management Act 1970* with the modifications specified in the Schedule to the regulations. Although some of the relevant provisions of the *Taxes Management Act 1970* have been substantially amended since 1986 (principally by *FA 1989*) it is thought that the correct view is that these subsequent amendments to the *Taxes Management Act 1970* itself are not to be taken into account for the purposes of the regulations (*Willows v Lewis Ch D [1982] STC 141*). The regulations may now include provisions specifying the form or manner in which notices and information must be given to the Commissioners. [*FA 1989, s 177*]. Interest on overdue stamp duty reserve tax is charged at the rate applicable under *FA 1986, s 178*. [*Taxes Management Act 1970, s 86* and *The Stamp Duty Reserve Tax (Amendment) Regulations 1989 (SI 1989 No 1301)*].

73.10   **FURTHER TREATMENT**

Further mention of stamp duty reserve tax will be found in the following chapters

ADMINISTRATION (3)
BEARER INSTRUMENTS (13)
CLEARANCE SERVICES (22)

74.1 Surrenders

74 Surrenders

74.1 A fixed duty of **50p** is payable on a surrender except where the surrender is for a consideration in which case it may be dutiable under the head CONVEYANCE OR TRANSFER (28) on sale.

74.2 For surrenders of leases see 53.7 LEASES.

75 Trusts and Trustees

75.1 CREATION OF A TRUST

Any inter vivos trust which is recorded by a written declaration of trust attracts a fixed duty of 50p as a DECLARATION OF TRUST (31). A written declaration of trust in favour of a purchaser of property may attract ad valorem duty under the head CONVEYANCE OR TRANSFER (28) on sale (*Chesterfield Brewery Co v CIR QB, [1899] 2 QB 7*). The vesting by CONVEYANCE OR TRANSFER (28) of property by way of gift to trustees following a declaration of trust will attract a 50p duty under the 'conveyance or transfer of any kind not hereinbefore described' head unless the instrument is certified in accordance with regulations in which case it will be exempt from duty and the requirement to have the instrument adjudicated. [*The Stamp Duty (Exempt Instruments) Regulations 1987 (SI 1987 No 516) Category L*; and see *Category G*

128

for transfers to trustees of a marriage settlement]. (See 39 EXEMPT INSTRU-MENTS.) A trust created by a will does not attract the fixed 50p duty nor any ad valorem duty. [*SA, 1 Sch*].

75.2 APPOINTMENT AND RETIREMENT OF TRUSTEES

The fixed 50p duty formerly charged on the appointment of new trustees has been abolished. [*SA, 1 Sch; FA 1985, 24 Sch (b)*]. The vesting by CON-VEYANCE OR TRANSFER (28) of trust property in new trustees bears duty of a maximum of 50p [*SA, s 62*] unless the instrument is certified in accordance with regulations in which case it will be exempt from duty. [*The Stamp Duty (Exempt Instruments) Regulations 1987 (SI 1987 No 516) Category A*]. (See 39 EXEMPT INSTRUMENTS.) If vesting is not express but merely takes effect by virtue of *Trustee Act 1925, s 40* the additional duty is not in practice claimed.

Duty is also limited to 50p on a CONVEYANCE OR TRANSFER (28) to give effect to the retirement of a trustee even though no new trustee is appointed [*FA 1902, s 9*], unless the instrument is certified in accordance with regulations in which case it is exempt from duty (see the regulations referred to above).

75.3 TRANSFERS OF TRUST PROPERTY OR INTERESTS

The CONVEYANCE OR TRANSFER (28) of trust property by trustees to a bene-ficiary will attract a fixed 50p duty under the head 'conveyance or transfer of any kind not hereinbefore described' unless the instrument is certified in accordance with regulations in which case it is exempt from duty. [*The Stamp Duty (Exempt Instruments) Regulations 1987 (SI 1987 No 516) Category F*]. (See 39 EXEMPT INSTRUMENTS.)

A transaction in trust interests by beneficiaries may attract ad valorem duty under the head CONVEYANCE OR TRANSFER (28) on sale (see e.g. *Oughtred v CIR HL, [1960] AC 206*—release of reversionary interest). If the trust property includes *chargeable securities* a STAMP DUTY RESERVE TAX (73) charge may arise if a duly stamped instrument is not created within two months of the transaction in trust interests, depending upon the nature of the bene-ficiary's interest in the trust.

75.4 VARIATION OF TRUSTS

As mentioned in 75.3 above the variation of an interest under a trust may involve a liability to ad valorem duty. However, an undertaking by solicitors with regard to stamping is no longer required to be included in an order made under the *Variation of Trusts Act 1958. Practice Note, [1966] 1 All ER 672* was withdrawn on 31 July 1989. Orders confined to the lifting of protective trusts are not liable to duty and need not be presented to the Stamp Office. Orders effecting a voluntary disposition inter vivos will attract a fixed 50p duty under the head 'conveyance or transfer of any kind not hereinbefore described' unless the order is certified in accordance with the regulations mentioned above (Category L). Orders which contain declarations of trust but effect no dis-position of the trust property are liable to 50p fixed duty under the head DECLARATION OF TRUST (31). [*Practice Direction (Chancery: Stamp Duty on Orders under the Variation of Trusts Act 1958) (3/89)*].

75.5   Trusts and Trustees

75.5 REVOCATION OF TRUST

The head of charge 'Revocation of any trust etc.' has been abolished. [*SA, 1 Sch; FA 1985, 24 Sch*].

75.6 CONSTRUCTIVE TRUSTS

Under an agreement for sale, a constructive trust arises for the purchaser, but this does not amount to a CONVEYANCE OR TRANSFER (28) of the property liable to stamp duty (*G Angus & Co CA, (1889) 23 QBD 579*). Agreements for sale may now be liable by virtue of *SA, s 59* (see 6 AGREEMENT FOR SALE).

75.7 MAINTENANCE FUNDS FOR HISTORIC BUILDINGS

No stamp duty is charged on an instrument whereby property leaves a settlement, if as a result of the property (or part of it) entering another settlement exemption from inheritance tax under *IHTA 1984, 4 Sch 9(1), 17(1)* is available, or only a reduced inheritance tax charge arises under *IHTA 1984, 4 Sch 9(4), 17(4)*. This does not apply where property leaves one settlement for another settlement by virtue of the instrument itself. Where only part of the property becomes comprised in the other settlement then stamp duty may be chargeable on the instrument in respect of the other part. The total or partial exemption is available only if the instrument is adjudicated (see 2 ADJUDICATION). [*FA 1980, s 98*].

---

76   Underwriting

76.1   An underwriting agreement is capable of attracting STAMP DUTY RESERVE TAX (73) as an agreement to transfer *chargeable securities* depending upon how it is worded. To avoid this problem the agreement should provide for the lead underwriter to procure purchasers, or failing this to purchase for himself only those shares not otherwise taken up by the public or the existing shareholders. Such a provision avoids any suggestion that the underwriting agreement is an agreement to transfer *chargeable securities* because at the date of the agreement it is not known whether the underwriter will be required to take-up any shares and if so, how many shares he will be required to take. Sub-underwriting agreements are in a similar position.

76.2   STAMP DUTY RESERVE TAX (73) should therefore only arise in relation to existing shares which the underwriter has to take-up and for which a duly stamped instrument of transfer is not produced within two months.

77   Unit Trusts

Note. Stamp duty and stamp duty reserve tax on the transfer of units in a unit trust scheme was to be abolished from a date to be appointed by statutory instrument. [*FA 1990, ss 108–111*]. But see 1.1 INTRODUCTION.

77.1 The head of charge 'Unit Trust Instrument' inserted in *SA, 1 Sch* by *FA 1962, s 30(1)*, was abolished by *FA 1988, s 140*. This former charge applied on the creation of a unit trust scheme and on later occasions when further property became trust property represented by units. The trust deed or other instrument creating or recording a unit trust is now liable to a fixed 50p duty under the head of charge 'Declaration of Trust'. [*SA, 1 Sch*]. (See 75 TRUSTS AND TRUSTEES.)

In general, transfers of units in a *unit trust scheme* (see 77.3 below) are treated as transfers of stock, liable to ad valorem duty under the head CONVEYANCE OR TRANSFER (28) on sale (see 77.2 below). Unit trust bearer certificates are chargeable under the head BEARER INSTRUMENTS (13).

77.2 **TRANSFERS OF UNITS**

(*a*) **Sales etc.** can be effected by direct transfer from one unit holder to another. An authority given by a unit holder to the trustees or managers to treat some other person as interested in a unit is deemed to be a conveyance or transfer, liable under the head 'CONVEYANCE OR TRANSFER (28) on sale', or 'conveyance or transfer of any kind not hereinbefore mentioned' if not on sale. [*FA 1946, s 57(2)*].

(*b*) **Surrender** is effected by an authority given by a unit holder to the trustees or managers to treat him as no longer interested in the unit and not requiring them to treat another person as so interested. This is treated as a transfer to the managers and is deemed to be a CONVEYANCE OR TRANSFER (28) on sale. [*FA 1946, s 57(3)*].

This provision was applied to the surrender to the managers of units in one portfolio for conversion into units in another portfolio managed by the same managers and established under the same trust deed. Ad valorem duty was therefore charged on the conversion form (*Arbuthnot Financial Services Ltd v CIR, Ch D, [1985] STC 211*). This case was decided under the pre-*FSA 1986* definition of *unit trust scheme*. See 77.4 below.

(*c*) **Resale of surrendered units** can be effected by an authority given by the managers to the trustees under a power arising from a previous transfer to them to treat a person as entitled to a unit. It is treated as a CONVEYANCE OR TRANSFER (28) unless the managers are acting to give effect to a transmission by operation of law. [*FA 1946, s 57(4)*].

(*d*) **Resale within two months of surrender.** The duty on a transfer by the managers under a power arising from the transfer to them of a unit within the preceding two months is 50p. [*FA 1946, s 54(3)*].

(*e*) **Surrender and extinction of units.** Duty paid on a transfer to the managers will be refunded if within two months after the transfer the trustees and the managers jointly certify that

(i) the certificate in respect of the unit has been cancelled;

(ii) in consequence, a part of the trust property has been realised;

(iii) the unit is extinguished and the managers have no right to transfer a unit in lieu.

[*FA 1946, s 54(4)*].

(*f*) **Units in gilt-edged etc. trusts.** No duty is payable on transfers of units in an authorised unit trust under the terms of which the funds of the trust cannot be invested

(i) in such a way that income arises to the trustees which will be taxable other than under Schedule C as profits arising from UK public revenue dividends or under Schedule D, Case III; and

(ii) in any investment which would bear ad valorem duty on transfer.

[*FA 1980, s 101*, as substituted by *FA 1989, s 174*].

This exemption applies to unit trusts which invest principally in UK Government stocks etc.

77.3 UNIT TRUST SCHEME

The definition of *unit trust scheme* has been changed by the *FSA 1986*. [*FA 1987, s 48(a)*]. A *unit trust scheme* is now defined as *a collective investment scheme* under which the property in question is held on trust for the participants. [*FA 1946, s 57(1); FSA 1986, s 75(8)*]. A *collective investment scheme* is in turn defined as any arrangements with respect to property of any description, including money, the purpose or effect of which is to enable persons taking part in the arrangements (whether by becoming owners of the property or any part of it or otherwise) to participate in or receive profits or income arising from the acquisition, holding, management or disposal of the property or sums paid out of such profits or income. [*FSA 1986, s 75(1)*]. The arrangements in question must be such that the participants have no day-to-day control over the management of the property in question, whether or not they have the right to be consulted or to give directions. The arrangements must also have one or both of the following characteristics:

(*a*) the contributions of participants and the profits or income out of which payments are to be made to them are pooled;

(*b*) the property in question is managed as a whole by or on behalf of the operator of the scheme.

[*FSA 1986, s 78(2)(3)*].

77.4 Where arrangements provide for the pooling of contributions, profits and income as in (*a*) above in relation to separate parts of the property in

132

question, the arrangements are not a *single* unit trust scheme unless the participants are entitled to exchange rights in one part of it for another. [*FSA 1986, s 75(4)*]. It would seem that where there is a right of exchange the arrangements are a *single* unit trust scheme (see 77.2(*b*) above).

77.5 Arrangements are not a *unit trust scheme* if

(*a*) the property (other than cash awaiting investment) consists of shares or stock of a company, debentures etc., certificates representing securities, government and public securities, share warrants etc., units in a separate unit trust and long-term insurance contracts; and

(*b*) each participant is the owner of part of that property and is entitled to withdraw it at any time; and

(*c*) the contributions and profits as income are not pooled and the property is managed as a whole only because the parts of the property belonging to different participants are not bought and sold separately except where a person becomes or ceases to be a participant.

[*FSA 1986, s 75(5)*].

77.6 The following are also excluded from the definition of *unit trust scheme*:

(*a*) arrangements operated by a person otherwise than by way of business;

(*b*) arrangements where each participant carries on a business other than an investment business and enters into the arrangements for commercial purposes related to that business;

(*c*) arrangements where each of the participants is a body corporate in the same group as the operator;

(*d*) arrangements where

(i) each of the participants is a bona fide employee or former employee (or the wife, husband, widow, widower, child or step-child under the age of 18 of such employee or former employee) of a body corporate in the same group as the operator; and

(ii) the property consists of shares or debentures in or of a member of that group;

(*e*) arrangements where the receipt of the participants' contributions constitutes the acceptance of deposits in the course of a business which is a deposit-taking business for the purposes of the *Banking Act 1979* and does not constitute a transaction prescribed for the purposes of *Sec 2* of that Act by Treasury regulations;

(*f*) franchise arrangements;

(*g*) arrangements where the predominant purpose is to enable participants to share in the use or enjoyment of particular property or to make its use or enjoyment available gratuitously to others;

(*h*) arrangements where the rights or interests of the participants are investments consisting of certificates representing securities;

(*j*) arrangements for the provision of clearance services and which are operated by an authorised person, a recognised clearing house or a recognised investment exchange;

(*k*) contracts of insurance;

(*l*) occupational pension schemes.

[*FSA 1986, s 75(8)*].

Common investment arrangements made by the trustees of exempt approved schemes within *FA 1970, s 21(1)* solely for the purposes of such schemes are excluded. [*FA 1981, s 110*].

Building societies, industrial or provident societies, friendly societies and bodies corporate other than open-ended investment companies are not to be regarded as a *unit trust scheme*. [*FSA 1986, s 75(7)*].

77.7 The Treasury may by regulations provide that any scheme shall be treated as not being a *unit trust scheme*. [*FA 1946, s 57(1A)(1B)*]. Regulations have been made excluding limited partnerships registered under the *Limited Partnerships Act 1907*, profit sharing schemes approved under *ICTA 1988, s 186* and a scheme made by the Lord Chancellor under the *Administration of Justice Act 1982* from the unit trust regime. [*The Stamp Duty and Stamp Duty Reserve Tax (Definitions of Unit Trust Scheme) Regulations 1988 (SI 1988 No 268) and SI 1992 No 197*]. Enterprise zone property trusts, however, continue to be treated as unit trust schemes. (See Inland Revenue Press Release, 23 December 1987.)

77.8 MISCELLANEOUS

(*a*) Any reference to stock in the stamp duty legislation includes a reference to unit trust units. [*FA 1946, s 54(1)*]. Therefore the transfer of units attracts the reduced rate of ad valorem duty on sale of 50p per £100 or part £100. The CERTIFICATE OF VALUE (19) exemption is not available and an agreement for the sale of units is not chargeable with duty under *SA, s 59*.

(*b*) Any reference to a stock certificate to bearer includes a certificate to bearer under a *unit trust scheme*. [*FA 1946, s 54(1)*]. Unit trust bearer certificates are thus within the head BEARER INSTRUMENTS (13) as inland or overseas bearer instruments as the case may be.

(*c*) Units in a *unit trust scheme* are chargeable securities for the purposes of STAMP DUTY RESERVE TAX (73) and '*unit*' and '*unit trust scheme*' have the same meanings as in stamp duty. [*FA 1986, s 99(3)(9)*]. No tax arises on an agreement to transfer units to the managers nor does tax arise on an agreement to transfer a unit if at the time of the agreement all the trustees under the scheme are resident outside the UK and the unit is not registered in a register kept in the UK by or on behalf of the trustees. [*FA 1986, s 90(1)(2)*].

---

78   VAT and Stamp Duty

78.1   Stamp duty is charged on the consideration or rent including any value added tax (*Glenrothes D.C. v IRC [1994] STC 74*). This has always been the position although before the major extension of the standard rate of value added tax to transactions involving buildings and land by *Finance Act 1989 s 18* and *3 Sch* the point rarely arose due to land and share transactions being generally exempt from value added tax.

78.2   However, the application of the CONTINGENCY PRINCIPLE (26) to a transaction which is capable of being a standard-rated supply for value added tax purposes is not so straightforward. It is clear that on a standard-rated sale of freehold land stamp duty will be charged on the conveyance according to the value added tax inclusive consideration. Where the consideration is uncertain and depends on the happening of a contingency, but a maximum, minimum or basic price can be ascertained, stamp duty is charged by the Stamp Office on that ascertainable amount plus the hypothetical value added tax that would have been chargeable on that amount under the CONTINGENCY PRINCIPLE (26). In other words, the Stamp Office take the view that the potential value added tax arising as a result of the possible exercise of the election to waive exemption is within the scope of the CONTINGENCY PRINCIPLE (26).

78.3   The major change in the value added tax chargeable on supplies relating to buildings and land made by *FA 1989, s 18* and *3 Sch* was the introduction of a mandatory value added tax charge on the sale of new commercial property. In addition, owners were given the option of charging value added tax on sales of old commercial property, and on leases of commercial property. The Inland Revenue published a Statement of Practice (SP 11/91) on 12 September 1991 dealing with the interaction between stamp duty and value added tax. This revised and replaced the earlier Statement of Practice of 22 July 1991 (SP 6/91). Although SP 11/91 contains the official view it should not be assumed that it is correct in all respects and in appropriate cases it may be open to challenge. SP 11/91 may be summarised as follows:

78.4   VAT and Stamp Duty

(*a*) For stamp duty purposes the amount or value of the consideration for sale is the gross amount inclusive of value added tax. Therefore where value added tax is chargeable on the sale of new non-residential property, stamp duty will be charged on the value added tax inclusive consideration.

(*b*) Sales of non-residential property, other than new buildings are generally exempt from value added tax. These include sales of old buildings, the assignment of existing leases and the creation of new leases in old or new property. However, the vendor can elect to waive the exemption. Where the election has been exercised at the time of the transaction, stamp duty is chargeable on the price, premium or rent inclusive of value added tax. Where the election has not been exercised at that time, value added tax should similarly be included in any payments to which an election could still apply for the purpose of calculating stamp duty unless there is a covenant or undertaking binding the vendor or lessor not to waive the exemption.

(*c*) For documents executed before 1 August 1991, the Stamp Office did not seek to include the value added tax element in the stamp duty charge in cases where an election to waive the exemption from value added tax had not yet been exercised. This practice has now altered for documents executed on or after 1 August 1991.

(*d*) Where value added tax is charged on the rent under a lease, and is treated as rent by the lease, stamp duty is charged on the value added tax inclusive figure. If the lease provides for payment of value added tax on the rent otherwise than as rent, stamp duty is charged on the value added tax element as consideration payable periodically. [*SA, s 56*]. In both cases the rate of value added tax in force at the date of execution of the lease is used. Because *SA, s 56* charges duty on a notional sum equivalent to the value added tax payable over the shorter of 20 years or the term of the lease this can increase the stamp duty charge significantly and means it will nearly always be cheaper to reserve value added tax as part of the rent rather than as a separate sum.

(*e*) Where there is a formal deed of variation or similar document varying the terms of the original lease so as to provide for payment of value added tax by way of additional rent, further stamp duty may be payable. [*SA, s 77(5)*].

(*f*) Paragraphs (*b*) to (*e*) above also apply to an AGREEMENT FOR LEASE (5) if that is to be stamped.

78.4   In response to the difficulties which SP 11/91 caused some practitioners, the Institute of Chartered Accountants in England and Wales issued a guidance note based on questions submitted by the Tax Faculty to the Stamp Office (Tax 19/92 Guidance Note). The Guidance Note may be summarised as follows:

(*a*) **VAT groups.** A lease granted between companies in the same value added tax group [*Value Added Tax Act 1994, s 43*] is assessed by reference to the premium (if any) and rents reserved by reference to the value added tax exclusive sums whether or not an election to waive exemption is in place on the property at the date of the grant.

(*b*) **VAT not recoverable as rent.** Where a lease is either silent as to the ability of the landlord to charge value added tax or states that value added tax is not recoverable by the landlord, the Stamp Office regard the CONTINGENCY PRINCIPLE (26) to be in point because the landlord, by virtue of *Value Added Tax Act 1994, 10 Sch 2*, could still elect to waive exemption from value added tax at any time during the term granted. As such, value added tax on rent would still form part of the consideration for the enjoyment of the premises in the same way that the payment of value added tax on a sale forms part of the consideration for the thing sold. The stamp duty chargeable on a document, and accordingly the CONTINGENCY PRINCIPLE (26), must be applied at the time the lease is executed. It is immaterial that the lease specifically states that value added tax is not recoverable by the landlord.

(*c*) **Property exchanges.** Where equality money is given or received on an exchange and neither property is subject to value added tax, stamp duty is payable on the equality money. [*SA, s 73*]. Value added tax is however capable of forming part of the stampable consideration paid or agreed to be paid for equality where both or either freehold properties are subject to a value added tax charge. [Note: *SA, s 73* was amended by *FA 1994, s 241*].

(*d*) **Split-purpose buildings.** Where a landlord has the right to waive exemption on part only of the rent, stamp duty is charged only on the value added tax on that part of the rent. Examples include a shop with a flat above and a building where a certificate of qualifying use has been issued in relation to part of the building.

(*e*) **Sub-sales.** In a sub-sale, A sells to B who sells to C and the transfer of title is completed by a single conveyance from A to C. Stamp duty is charged only on the price paid by C. If that price is subject to value added tax, stamp duty is charged on the value added tax inclusive amount. Any value added tax element in the price paid by B to A is ignored unless that initial transaction is also stampable.

(*f*) **Transfer of going concern.** Where a lease is transferred as one of the assets of a business transferred as a going concern, it falls outside the scope of value added tax provided the conditions set out in *article 5* of the *Value Added Tax (Special Provisions) Order 1992 (SI 1992 No 3192)* are satisfied. In such a case the charge to ad valorem duty will be confined to the value added tax exclusive amounts, the transaction being a non-supply for the purposes of value added tax.

(*g*) **Binding agreement not to waive exemption.** Where there is a binding agreement between the parties not to exercise the option to waive exemption at the date of the grant of a lease, ad valorem duty will be assessed on the value added tax exclusive rents reserved in the lease.

(*h*) **Agreement for leases.** Where an AGREEMENT FOR LEASE (5) is stamped under the CONTINGENCY PRINCIPLE (26) on the basis that an election to waive exemption might subsequently be made but between the date of the agreement and the grant of the lease a binding agreement is made not to waive the exemption, the lease is denoted with the duty paid on the agreement. There is no provision for a refund of duty even though the lease would have been stamped on the (lesser) value added tax exclusive basis.

(*j*) **Bare land.** The Statement of Practice relates not only to buildings but also to bare land.

---

79   Practical Materials

STATUTORY DECLARATION

(in connection with a claim for exemption from stamp duty under section 42 Finance Act 1930 on a transfer made between companies within the same group)

I, [name of declarant   ] of [address of declarant   ]
do SOLEMNLY AND SINCERELY DECLARE as follows:

1   DEFINITIONS

In this declaration:

"ordinary share capital" means all the issued share capital of the body corporate concerned other than capital the holders of which have a right to a dividend at a fixed rate but have no other right to share in the profits of the body corporate

"section 42" means section 42 Finance Act 1930 as amended by section 27 Finance Act 1967 and section 149 Finance Act 1995

"the transferor" means [name of transferor]

"the transferee" means [name of transferee]

138

"the transferred assets" means [the assets] described in and transferred by the transfer instrument

"the transfer instrument" means the [description of instrument] dated [   ] and made between [the transferor] and [the transferee], a certified copy of which is exhibited to this declaration marked "[   ]"

[*"the parent"* means [name of parent if relevant]]

[*"relevant intermediate company"* means a company through which it is necessary to trace ownership in order to establish that the transferor and the transferee are associated for the purpose of section 42]

2 POSITION OF DECLARANT

I am [a director] [the company secretary] of [the parent] [the transferor] [the transferee].

3 CLAIM FOR EXEMPTION

A claim for exemption under section 42 is made hereby in respect of the transfer instrument the original of which is submitted for adjudication with this declaration.

4 DETAILS OF COMPANIES

Relevant details of the transferor and the transferee [and of the parent] [and of any relevant intermediate companies] at the date of the transfer instrument are as follows:-

A. TRANSFEROR

1 Registered number	:	[ ]
2 Date of incorporation	:	[ ]
3 Place of incorporation	:	[ ]
4 Authorised share capital	:	[ ]
5 Issued ordinary share capital	:	[ ]
6 Issued non-ordinary share capital	:	[ ]
7 Shareholders		

No of shares	Ordinary/ Non Ordinary-Shares	Registered Holder	Beneficial Owner if Different
[ ]	[Ordinary/ Non-Ordinary]	[ ]	[ ]

139

B.   TRANSFEREE

1   Registered number   :   [   ]
2   Date of incorporation   :   [   ]
3   Place of incorporation   :   [   ]
4   Authorised share capital   :   [   ]
5   Issued ordinary share capital   :   [   ]
6   Issued non-ordinary share capital   :   [   ]
7   Shareholders

No of shares	Ordinary/ Non Ordinary-Shares	Registered Holder	Beneficial Owner if Different
[ ]	[Ordinary/ Non-Ordinary]	[ ]	[ ]

[C. PARENT

1   Registered number   :   [   ]
2   Date of incorporation   :   [   ]
3   Place of incorporation   :   [   ]
4   Authorised share capital   :   [   ]
5   Issued share capital   :   [   ]]

[D.   [   ] LIMITED ("[   ]")

1   Registered number   :   [   ]
2   Date of incorporation   :   [   ]
3   Place of incorporation   :   [   ]
4   Authorised share capital   :   [   ]
5   Issued ordinary share capital   :   [   ]
6   Issued non-ordinary share capital   :   [   ]]
7   Shareholders

No of shares	Ordinary/ Non Ordinary-Shares	Registered Holder	Beneficial Owner if Different
[ ]	[Ordinary/ Non-Ordinary]	[ ]	[ ]

[E.   REPEAT AS NECESSARY]

A chart illustrating the relationship between the companies concerned is exhibited to this declaration marked "[   ]".

5 LIQUIDATION

Neither the transferor nor the transferee [nor the parent] [nor any relevant intermediate company] was at the date of the transfer instrument or is now in liquidation.

6 RELATIONSHIP BETWEEN COMPANIES

For the purposes of section 42, at the date of the transfer instrument and of this declaration

[the [transferee] [transferor] was the beneficial owner of not less than seventy five per cent of the ordinary share capital of the [transferor] [transferee].]

– OR –

[the parent was the beneficial owner of not less than seventy five per cent of the ordinary share capital of the transferor and of the transferee.]

[A certified copy of an extract from the register of members of the [transferor] [transferee] [each relevant intermediate company] is exhibited to this declaration marked "[   ]".]

[A declaration of trust evidencing the beneficial ownership of [   ] in the shares in [   ] is exhibited to this declaration marked "[   ]".]

7 CONTINUANCE OF RELATIONSHIP

The [parent] [transferor] [transferee] has no present intention to undertake any transaction which would cause the transferor and the transferee to cease to be associated for the purpose of section 42.

8 CONTINUANCE OF OWNERSHIP

The transferee has no present intention to dispose of its beneficial ownership of the transferred assets.

9 CONSIDERATION

The consideration for the transfer of the transferred assets [was [   ]] [is set out in the transfer instrument] [is set out in an agreement dated [   ] and made between [amongst others] the transferor and the transferee a copy of which is exhibited to this declaration marked "[   ]"]

141

[The consideration was provided by the transferee in money out of its own resources].

[The consideration was left outstanding on an inter-company loan which is repayable to the transferor by the transferee on [date] OR [demand] is unsecured and bears interest at the rate of [   ] and is otherwise on the terms set out in resolutions of the board of directors of the transferor and the transferee respectively. Certified extracts from the minutes of a board meeting of the transferor, held on [   ] and from the minutes of a board meeting of the transferee held on [   ] are exhibited to this declaration and marked "[   ]" respectively.]

[A copy of the transferee's last available balance sheet dated [   ] is exhibited marked "[   ]".]

[The consideration was paid out of a borrowing by the transferee from [   ] Bank plc under overdraft facilities provided to the transferee. Copies of the correspondence under which this facility was requested and granted [and the loan agreement] are exhibited to this declaration marked "[   ]".]

10   SECTION 27(3) FINANCE ACT 1967

The transfer instrument was not executed in pursuance of or in connection with such an arrangement as is mentioned in section 27(3) Finance Act 1967.

AND I MAKE THIS SOLEMN DECLARATION CONSCIENTIOUSLY BELIEVING THE SAME TO BE TRUE AND BY VIRTUE OF THE STATUTORY DECLARATIONS ACT 1835.

DECLARED at [   ]   )
)
on [   ]   )   . . . .
)
)   Signature of declarant
Before me,   )

. . . .
Solicitor/Commissioner for Oaths

MARKING ON EXHIBITS

This is the Exhibit marked "[   ]" referred to in the statutory declaration of [   ], declared before me this [   ] day of [   ].

. . . .

Solicitor/Commissioner for Oaths

INTER GROUP RELIEF FROM STAMP DUTY
(SECTION 42 FINANCE ACT 1930)

This leaflet is a short guide on how you can claim relief from paying stamp duty in respect of documents executed between companies in the same group. It does not cover all the points that can arise, so if any further information is required please contact Worthing Stamp Office Telephone 01903 288835 or The Stamp Office (Scotland) Telephone 0131 556 8511.

The purpose of this guide is to tell you what information we need so that your claim can be processed quickly.

STAMP DUTY RELIEF IN RESPECT OF INTER GROUP TRANSACTIONS

A document which has the effect of passing a beneficial interest in property between "bodies corporate" which would normally be liable to ad valorem duty as a conveyance or transfer on sale will be exempt from this duty provided a claim for relief is made successfully under the provisions of Section 42 Finance Act 1930 as amended by Section 27 Finance Act 1967 and Section 149 Finance Act 1995. Section 151 Finance Act 1995 also extends the relief to Agreements for Leases and Leases which are executed inter group on or after 1 May 1995.

TRANSFER OF BENEFICIAL INTEREST

If relief from conveyance or transfer on sale duty or lease duty is being sought, a chargeable consideration must be provided and in the former case there must also have been the transfer of a beneficial interest.

Relief would not be available on documents which transferred to or from a "body corporate" which acted in a trustee capacity, eg for a group pension scheme. Equally relief would not be available if a mortgagee under power of sale were to transfer property to an associated company.

WHAT IS A "BODY CORPORATE"?

A "body corporate" is one which has perpetual succession and a legal personality distinct from that of its members. In the United Kingdom a body corporate would include companies with limited or unlimited liability, companies limited by guarantee, charter companies and bodies created by statute. The relief is not restricted to a body corporate situated in the United Kingdom and is available to any non UK "body corporate".

ASSOCIATED BODIES CORPORATE

Bodies corporate have to be associated as follows:

a.   Prior to 1 May 1995, a body corporate had to be the beneficial owner of not less than 90% of the **issued** share capital of the other party to the transaction or a third body corporate had to be the beneficial owner of not less than 90% of the issued share capital of both the transferor and transferee companies.

W2161-5-95(1) F136

b. **For documents executed on or after 1 May 1995 bodies corporate will be associated if one is the beneficial owner of not less than 75% of the issued ordinary share capital** of the other, or a third body corporate is the beneficial owner of not less than **75% of the issued ordinary share capital** of each body corporate. **Ordinary share capital are shares of whatever description except those which are entitled to a Fixed Dividend but have no other right to a share in the profits of the body corporate.**

In either case the relationship can be direct or through intermediate companies. So a claim can be made for transactions between A and B if there is a direct relationship or between A and C which are both associated with A provided that the relationship with A meets the required test.

DOES STAMP DUTY RELIEF UNDER SECTION 42 FINANCE ACT 1930 APPLY IN RESPECT OF AGREEMENTS FOR LEASES AND LEASES?

Yes, in respect of documents executed on or after 1 May 1995.

WHAT IS THE POSITION IF AN AGREEMENT FOR LEASE WAS EXECUTED BEFORE AND THE LEASE WAS EXECUTED ON OR AFTER 1 MAY 1995

A Lease executed on or after 1 May 1995 would not bring an Agreement for Lease executed prior to 1 May 1995 within the relieving provisions offered by Section 151 Finance Act 1995. The Agreement would be chargeable to duty under Section 75(1) Stamp Act 1891.

WHAT IS THE POSITION IF A BUSINESS SALE AGREEMENT AND THE TRANSFER WERE EXECUTED BEFORE AND AFTER 1 MAY 1995?

A Business Sale Agreement executed prior to 1 May 1995 might have been granted exemption from stamp duty under Section 42 Finance Act 1930, by reason of the association of 90% of the **issued share capital**. An exemption for supplementary documents executed on or after 1 May 1995 would not however be available if the relationship test of 75% of the issued ordinary share capital did not exist at the date of the transfer document.

If however a Business Sale Agreement was executed prior to 1 May 1995 and did not qualify for relief, transfer documents executed on or after 1 May 1995 may qualify for relief if the relationship test of **75% of the issued ordinary share capital** did exist at the date of the supplementary document (subject of course to the other conditions being satisfied).

HOW CAN I CLAIM STAMP DUTY RELIEF?

A Statutory Declaration has to be completed which can be sworn both, within or outside the United Kingdom, before an Official authorised to administer oaths. The person swearing the Statutory Declaration should be a board member of the immediate parent company or a solicitor acting on its behalf.

W2161-5-95(2) F136

WHERE SHOULD STATUTORY DECLARATIONS BE SENT?

When completed your original Statutory Declaration together with your original documents (and exhibits) should be sent to:

Worthing Stamp Office
Ridgeworth House
Liverpool Gardens
WORTHING
West Sussex   BN11 1XP

01903 288835
DX 3799 WORTHING 1

or for companies registered in Scotland or Northern Ireland:

The Stamp Office (Scotland)
Mulberry House
16 Picardy Place
EDINBURGH   EH1 3NF

0131 556 8511
DX ED 303 EDINBURGH 1

COMPLETION OF THE STATUTORY DECLARATION

To enable claims for relief from stamp duty under Section 42 Finance Act 1930 or Section 151 Finance Act 1995 to be dealt with, the following information should be provided in the Statutory Declaration:

1. it should state that a claim under Section 42 Finance Act 1930 as amended by Section 27 Finance Act 1967 and Section 149 Finance Act 1995 is made in respect of specified documents for Conveyance on Sale duty and/or Section 151 Finance Act 1995 if in respect of Lease duty. Copies of the relevant documents should be attached to the Statutory Declaration;

2. give details at the dates of all documents of the authorised and issued share capital of the subsidiary companies and of any intermediate companies and whether any class of share carries a right only to a Fixed Dividend and no other share in the profits. (If the parties to the transaction are indirectly associated a family tree should also be supplied);

3. state whether any of the bodies corporate is in liquidation;

4. show details of shares held by each shareholder in each subsidiary company and any intermediate company. If the relationship between companies is dependant upon shares held by nominees, documentary evidence evidencing the beneficial ownership of the shares should also be provided;

5. say whether it is intended that:

    a. the relationship required by the legislation is to be maintained;

    b. the Transferee body corporate will retain the beneficial ownership of the transferred property;

W2161-5-95(3) F136

6. give the amount of the consideration and whether it was satisfied from cash resources, through an Inter Company Loan Account or by way of a Third Party Loan. If the latter, details of any conditions imposed on the loan should be given;

7. give an assurance that none of the documents were executed in pursuance of or in connection with an arrangement described in Section 27(3) Finance Act 1967.

The Statutory Declaration should be sent with:

- the original of all documents referred to in the Declaration;

- certified copies of all the documents;

- a certified extract from the Register of Members of all subsidiary and intermediate companies;

and where appropriate:

- a copy of the latest accounts of the Transferee company if the consideration was provided from cash resources;

- copies of any agreement with a third party relating to the provision of consideration;

- copies of correspondence, agreements, board minutes etc if the relationship between the parties or the ownership of the transferred property were not to continue.

THE STAMP OFFICE
MAY 1995

ADJ 428(D)

W2161-5-95(4) F136

Relief from Stamp Duty under S75/76/77 Finance Act 1986 in connection with Company Reconstructions

1. Following the repeal of S 55 FA 1927 & S 78/79 FA 1985, we have reviewed our requirements in connection with claims for relief under S 75, 76 & 77 FA 1986. These notes deal only with the procedure to be followed in submitting a claim.

2. A statutory declaration is no longer required. A claim must be made in a letter signed by a responsible officer of the acquiring company (eg the secretary or a director) or the company's professional advisers.

3. The information needed to determine whether relief is due depends on the section under which relief is being claimed. The following 2 paragraphs indicate our requirements. An entry of 'yes' in the grid means that the information must be supplied.

4. Information to be included in the letter claiming relief:

	Section of FA 1986 under which claim is being made		
	S 75	S 76	S 77
a. i. the name and registered number of the acquiring company at the date of the agreement or offer	Yes	Yes	Yes
ii. the authorised and issued capital of the acquiring company at the date of the agreement or offer	Yes	No	Yes
b. i. the name and registered number of the target company at the date of the agreement or offer	Yes	Yes	Yes
ii. the authorised and issued capital of the target company at the date of the agreement or offer	Yes	Yes	Yes
c. details of the transaction	Yes	Yes	Yes
d. a statement of the consideration paid and how it was satisfied	Yes	Yes	Yes
e. reasons for the transaction, and whether an application for clearance under S 88 CGTA 1979 or S 707 ICTA 1988 has been made to the Board of Inland Revenue, if known	Yes	No	Yes
f. confirmation that the shares in the acquiring company have been issued to			
i. all the shareholders of the target company and that their names have been entered on the Register of Members	Yes	No	Yes
ii. to the target company or to all or any of its shareholders and that their names have been entered on the Register of Members	No	Yes	No

5. Supporting information which must accompany the claim for relief.

		Section of FA 1986 under which claim is being made		
		S 75	S 76	S 77
a.	a copy of the certificate of incorporation of all companies and all changes of names	Yes	Yes	Yes
b.	a list of all members of the target company immediately prior to the transaction certified by the Registrar (or a computerised print-out) detailing the shares held by each shareholder	Yes	Yes	Yes
c.	a list of all members of the acquiring company immediately after the transaction for which relief is claimed, certified by the Registrar (or a computerised print-out) detailing the shares held by each shareholder	Yes	No	Yes
d.	a copy of any application for clearance referred to at 4.e. above, together with copies of any correspondence with the Board of Inland Revenue; sufficient evidence must be supplied to enable the companies to be identified — such applications often refer to "Newco", 'Company A' etc	Yes	No	Yes
e.	The original agreement or offer document	Yes	Yes	No
f.	A copy of the agreement or offer document	Yes	Yes	Yes
g.	The original instruments of transfer (plus copies for retention)	Yes	Yes	Yes
h.	A completed "apportionment" form Stamps No. 22	No	Yes	No

6. When forwarding your application please state any related Adjudication references known to you.

7. Precedent letters are available on application to the Adjudication Section.

Issued by The Stamp Office Adjudication Section Ridgeworth House Liverpool Gardens Worthing West Sussex BN11 1XP

W1Cs3-3-91-2 C

149

The Stamp Office

Worthing Stamp Office
Company Reorganisation Section
Ridgeworth House
Liverpool Gardens
Worthing
West Sussex BN11 1XP
Telephone: 01903 288
Fax: 01903 288848
DX 3799 Worthing 1
Manager: Walter Coughlin

The attached draft letter should be used when relief is claimed under S77 FA 1986. Completed claims should be sent to the above address.

Dear Sir

.... Limited/plc

Section 77 Finance Act 1986

1.   We act for .... Limited/plc ("the Acquiring Company").

2.   In connection with the transactions referred to below we hereby apply on behalf of the Acquiring Company for exemption from transfer duty under Section 77 Finance Act 1986.

3.   The Acquiring Company, whose registered office is at ....,
     was incorporated in [England] on ...., 19 ...... [under the Companies Act[s] 19 ...... [to 19 ......]
     with No ....] and immediately prior to .... 19 ...... the authorised share capital of the
     Acquiring Company was £ .... divided into [................ per cent. .... Preference Shares of
     .... each and] .... Ordinary Shares of .... each, of which [................ such Preference
     Shares and] .... such Ordinary Shares had been issued and were fully paid up]. A copy of the
     Certificate of Incorporation [and the Certificate of Incorporation on Change of Name] [is/are] enclosed
     marked "A".

4.   .... Limited/plc ("the Target Company"),
     whose registered office is at ...., was incorporated
     in [England] on ...., 19 ...... [under the Companies Act[s] 19 ...... [to 19 ......]
     with No ....] and immediately prior to .... 19 ...... the authorised share capital of the
     Target Company was £ .... divided into [................ per cent. .... Preference Shares of
     .... each and] .... Ordinary Shares of .... each, of which [................ such Preference
     Shares and] .... such Ordinary Shares had been issued and were fully paid up]. A copy of the
     Certificate of Incorporation [and the Certificate of Incorporation on Change of Name] [is/are] enclosed
     marked "B". A list of all members of the Target Company immediately prior to .... 19 ......,
     certified by the Registrars of the Target Company, is enclosed marked "C".

Inland
Revenue
The Stamp Office

[NOTE — A computerised print-out, which need not be certified, is acceptable (if available) instead of the list of members.]

5. The transactions referred to below were carried out in order that ... [set out briefly the reasons for the transactions]. [Note: if advance clearance was <u>not</u> obtained (see paragraph 12) then please give a <u>detailed</u> explanation of the bona fide commercial reasons for the transaction.]

6. By an Agreement dated .... 19 ..... and made between ....
    and .... ("the Shareholder[s]") (i) the Target Company (ii) and the Acquiring
    Company (iii) ("the Agreement"), it was provided (inter alia) that the Shareholder[s] should sell and the
    Acquiring Company should purchase the [respective] number[s] of [............ per cent. .... Preference
    Shares of .... each and] .... Ordinary Shares of .... each of the Target Company
    set out in [Clause ....: of/column[s] (...............) [and (...............) respectively] of Schedule ....
    to the Agreement (such Shares amounting in the aggregate to the whole of the issued share capital of
    the Target Company) and that as consideration for such sale the Acquiring Company should allot
    credited as fully paid to the Shareholders (being all the shareholders of the Target Company) [............... /
    the [respective] number[s] of] [................... per cent Preference shares of .... each and] Ordinary
    Shares of .... each of the Acquiring Company set out in [Clause .... of/column (............) of] such
    Schedule] ("the Consideration Shares"). A copy of the Agreement is enclosed marked "D".

7. The said sale was duly completed on .... 19 ...... when the Shareholders delivered to and
    in favour of the Acquiring Company duly executed transfers of the whole of the issued Shares of the
    Target Company. Immediately following such delivery one Ordinary Share of ....
    of .... was transferred to .... [jointly] as nominee[s] of
    the Acquiring Company in order that there could be the necessary minimum number of Members of the
    Target Company and a quorum of Members could be present at General Meetings of the Target
    Company. There was also delivered to the Acquiring Company the relevant Share Certificates.

8. At a Meeting of [a Committee of] the Directors of the Acquiring Company held on .... 19 ......
    the Consideration Shares (which had been created by Resolution No .... passed at the Extraordinary
    General Meeting held on .... 19 ......) were duly allotted to the Shareholders pursuant to the
    provisions of the Agreement. We enclose marked ["E"] [and ["F"] respectively] [a] certified [copy/copies]
    of the Resolution of the Directors of the Acquiring Company passed on .... 19 ......
    [appointing the said Committee and of the Resolution of the said Committee of the Directors] making
    such allotment. We also enclose marked ["D"] a certificate under the hand of Mr ....,
    [the senior official of the Registration Department of .... Limited/plc,

The Stamp Office is an Executive Office of the Inland Revenue

ADJ 473 (Cont)

W2221-5-95(2) 17

the Registrars] [the Company Secretary] of the Acquiring Company, confirming that the names of the respective allotees of the Consideration Shares have been entered in the Register of [Members of] the Acquiring Company in respect of the Consideration Shares together with a list of all members of the Acquiring Company immediately following the allotment, certified by [the Registrars] [the Company Secretary] of the Acquiring Company, marked "H".

[NOTE — A computerised print-out, which need not be certified, is acceptable (if available) instead of the list of members.]

9.   Immediately following the acquisition the authorised share capital of the Acquiring Company was £ .... divided into [............... per cent .... Preference Shares of .... each and] .... Ordinary Shares of .... each, of which [...................... such Preference Shares and] .... such Ordinary Shares had been issued and were fully paid up.

10.   It is confirmed that immediately following the acquisition the classes of shares in the Acquiring Company were in the same proportions as they had been in the Target Company immediately before the acquisition was made.

11.   It is confirmed that immediately following the acquisition the proportion of shares of any particular class in the Acquiring Company held by each shareholder was the same as the proportion of shares of that class in the Target Company held by him immediately before the acquisition was made.

12.   [An] [No] application(s) for clearance under [Section 138 or 139 TCGA 1992] [Section 707 ICTA 1988] [has/have] been made by the [Acquiring] [Target] Company. A copy of the application(s) [together with copies of correspondence with the Board of Inland Revenue] [are/is] enclosed marked ["J"]. [Note: if advance clearance was <u>not</u> obtained then please provide the information listed overleaf.]

13.   It is submitted that the acquisition was effected for bona fide commercial reasons and does not form part of a scheme or arrangement of which the main purpose, or one of the main purposes, is avoidance of liability to stamp duty, stamp duty reserve tax, income tax, corporation tax or capital gains tax and the appropriate conditions of Section 77 Finance Act 1986 have been complied with, and accordingly exemption from ad valorem stamp duty under the head "Conveyance or Transfer on Sale" is claimed in respect of the Agreement and the transfers executed pursuant thereto.

14.   We enclose for adjudication [describe document] together with [a] certified [copy/copies].

The Stamp Office is an Executive Office of the Inland Revenue

Inland
Revenue
The Stamp Office

Please telephone .... if you require any further information.

Yours faithfully

Information to be supplied if advance clearance was <u>not</u> obtained (see paragraphs 5 and 12 of the draft letter):

1.   a copy of the latest accounts of the target company;

2.   full details of any scheme or arrangement of which the acquisition of the target company forms a part;

3.   confirmation, if appropriate, that the shares in the target company are still held by the acquiring company and that there is no intention to dispose of them; and

4.   a <u>detailed</u> note of the bona fide commercial reasons for the acquisition.

The Stamp Office is an Executive Office of the Inland Revenue

ADJ 473(Cont)   W2221-5-95(4) 17

Inland Revenue
THE STAMP OFFICE
ADJUDICATION SECTION
Ridgeworth House   Liverpool Gardens
Worthing   West Sussex
BN11 1XP

The attached draft letter should be used when relief is claimed under S76 FA 1986. Completed claims should be sent to the above address.

Dear Sir

.... Limited/plc

Section 76 Finance Act 1986

1.   We act for .... Limited/plc ("the Acquiring Company").

2.   In connection with the transactions referred to below we hereby apply on behalf of the Acquiring Company for relief from transfer duty under Section 76 Finance Act 1986.

3.   The Acquiring Company, whose registered office is at ...., was incorporated in [England] on ...., 19 ...... [under the Companies Act[s] 19 ...... [to 19 ......] with No. ....] A copy of the Certificate of Incorporation [and the Certificate of Incorporation on Change of Name] [is/are] enclosed marked "A".

4.   .... Limited/plc ("the Target Company"), whose registered office is at ....,was incorporated in [England] on ...., 19 ...... [under the Companies Act[s] 19 ...... [to 19 ......] with No. ....] A copy of the Certificate of Incorporation [and the Certificate of Incorporation on Change of Name] [is/are] enclosed marked "B".

5.   By an Agreement dated .... 19 ...... and made between the Target Company (i) and the Acquiring Company (ii) ("the Agreement"), it was provided (inter alia) that the Target Company should sell and the Acquiring Company should purchase [the whole of] [part of] the undertaking of the Target Company as described in Schedule .... to the Agreement ("the Business") and that as consideration for such sale the Acquiring Company should allot credited as fully paid to the [Target Company] [holders of shares in the Target Company as specified in Schedule .... to the Agreement] [.........../the [respective] number[s] of] [Ordinary] Shares of .... each of the Acquiring Company set out in [Clause .... of/ column (...........) of] such Schedule] [such Shares amounting in aggregate to ....] ("the Consideration Shares") [and the Acquiring Company should make a cash payment of £ .... to the Target Company such sum not exceeding 10 per cent of the nominal value of the Consideration Shares so issued] [and the Acquiring Company would assume or discharge liabilities amounting to £ .... of the Target Company]. A copy of the Agreement is enclosed marked "C".

6. The said sale was duly completed on .... 19 ...... when the Target Company transferred the Business to the Acquiring Company.

7. At a Meeting of [a Committee of] the Directors of the Acquiring Company held on .... 19 ..... the Consideration Shares (which had been created by Resolution No. .... passed at the Extraordinary General Meeting held on .... 19 ......) were duly allotted to the [Target Company] [the holders of shares in the Target Company] pursuant to the provisions of the Agreement. We enclose marked ["D"] [and ["E"] respectively [a] certified [copy/copies] of the Resolution of the Directors of the Acquiring Company passed on .... 19 ...... [appointing the said Committee and of the Resolution of the said Committee of the Directors] making such allotment. We also enclose marked ["d"] a certificate under the hand of Mr .... , [the senior official of the Registration Department of .... Limited/plc, the Registrars] [the Company Secretary] of the Acquiring Company, confirming that the names of the respective allottees of the Consideration Shares have been entered in the Register of [Members of] the Acquiring Company in respect of the Consideration Shares.

8. By a Deed of Assignment dated .... 19 ...... and made between .... ("the Creditor(s)") (i) the Acquiring Company (ii) [and the Target Company (iii)] ("the Assignment") the Creditor(s) assigned to the Acquiring Company the debts owed by the Target Company to the Creditors as specified in Schedule .... to the Assignment, [the Creditor(s) being [(a) bank(s)] [(a) licensed deposit taker(s) recognised by the Inland Revenue as carrying on a bona fide banking business in the United Kingdom] [(a) trade creditor(s)]] [such debts having been incurred not less than 2 years before .... 19 ......, being the date upon which the Assignment was executed]] The original of the Assignment is enclosed (together with a copy) marked "G".

9. We submit that the appropriate conditions of section 76 of the Finance Act 1986 have been complied with and accordingly reduction in the rate of stamp duty under the head "Conveyance or Transfer on Sale" to 50p for every £100 or part of £100 of the amount or value of the consideration for the sale is claimed in respect of the transfers executed pursuant to the Agreement [and the Assignment].

10. We enclose for adjudication [describe document(s)] together with [a] certified [copy/copies].

Would you kindly telephone in the first instance M .... should you require any further information.

Yours faithfully

Inland Revenue
The Stamp Office
Adjudication Section
DX 3799 Worthing 1

Ridgeworth House
Liverpool Gardens
Worthing
West Sussex
BN11 1XP

FAX 0903 288848
Telephone (0903) 288

The attached draft letter should be used when relief is claimed under S75 FA 1986. Completed claims should be sent to the above address.

Dear Sir

.... Limited/plc

Section 75 Finance Act 1986

1.   We act for .... Limited/plc ("the Acquiring Company").

2.   In connection with the transactions referred to below we hereby apply on behalf of the Acquiring Company for exemption from transfer duty under Section 75 Finance Act 1986.

3.   The Acquiring Company, whose registered office is at ...., was incorporated in [England] on ...., 19 ..... [under the Companies Act[s] 19 ...... [to 19 ......] with No. ....] A copy of the Certificate of Incorporation [and the Certificate of Incorporation on Change of Name] [is/are] enclosed marked "A".

4.   .... Limited/plc ("the Target Company"), whose registered office is at .... ,was incorporated in [England] on .... , 19 ..... [under the Companies Act[s] 19 ...... [to 19 ......] with No. ....] A copy of the Certificate of Incorporation [and the Certificate of Incorporation on Change of Name] [is/are] enclosed marked "B". A list of all members of the Target Company immediately prior to .... 19 ......, certified by the Registrars of the Target Company, is enclosed marked "C".

[NOTE — A computerised print-out, which need not be certified, is acceptable (if available) instead of the list of members.]

5.   The Acquiring Company has acquired [the whole] [part of] the undertaking of the Target Company in pursuance of a scheme for the reconstruction of the Target Company in order that ... [set out briefly the reasons for the transactions].

ADJ 475   W4235-9-92(1) 56

6.   By an Agreement dated .... 19 ...... and made between the Target Company (i) and
      the Acquiring Company (ii) ("the Agreement"), it was provided (inter alia) that the Target Company
      should sell and the Acquiring Company should purchase the [whole of] [part of] the undertaking of the
      Target Company as described in Schedule .... to the Agreement ("the Business") in pursuance of a
      scheme for the reconstruction of the Target Company and that as consideration for such sale the
      Acquiring Company should allot credited as fully paid to all the shareholders of the Target Company
      [........................ /the [respective] number[s] of] [........................ per cent .... Preference Shares
      of .... each and] .... Ordinary Shares of .... each of the Acquiring Company set
      out in [Clause .... of/column (........................) of] such Schedule] ("the Consideration Shares").
      [In addition the Acquiring Company [assumed] [discharged] certain liabilities of the Acquired Company
      as specified in Schedule .... to the Agreement]. A copy of the Agreement is enclosed marked "D".

7.   The said sale was duly completed on .... 19 ...... when the Target Company transferred
      the Business to the Acquiring Company.

8.   At a Meeting of [a Committee of] the Directors of the Acquiring Company held on .... 19 ......
      the Consideration Shares (which had been created by Resolution No. .... passed at the Extraordinary
      General Meeting held on .... 19 ......) were duly allotted to the shareholders of the Target
      Company pursuant to the provisions of the Agreement. We enclose marked ["E"] [and ["F"] respectively]
      [a] certified [copy/copies] of the Resolution of the Directors of the Acquiring Company passed on
      .... 19 ...... [appointing the said Committee and of the Resolution of the said Committee
      of the Directors] making such allotment. We also enclosed marked ["G"] a certificate under the hand of
      Mr .... , [the senior official of the Registration Department of
      .... Limited/plc, the Registrars] [the Company
      Secretary] of the Acquiring Company, confirming that the names of the respective allotees of the
      Consideration Shares have been entered in the Register of [Members of] the Acquiring Company in
      respect of the Consideration Shares together with a list of all members of the Acquiring Company
      immediately following the allotment, certified by [the Registrars] [the Company Secretary] of the
      Acquiring Company, marked ["H"].

[NOTE — A computerised print-out, which does not have to be certified, is acceptable instead of the list
of members.]

9.   It is confirmed that, immediately after the Consideration Shares had been allotted:

      a.   each shareholder of the Target Company was also a shareholder of the Acquiring Company;

b.   each shareholder of the Acquiring Company was also a shareholder of the Target Company; and

c.   each shareholder held the same proportion of shares in the Target Company as that shareholder held in the Acquiring Company.

10.   [An] [No] application(s) for clearance under [Section 88 CGTA 1970] [Section 267 ICTA 1970] [has/have] been made by the [Acquiring] [Target] Company. A copy of the application(s) [together with copies of the correspondence with the Board of Inland Revenue] [are/is] enclosed marked ["I"].

11.   It is submitted that the acquisition was/is effected for bona fide commercial reasons and did not form part of a scheme or arrangement of which the main purpose, or one of the main purposes, is avoidance of liability to stamp duty, income tax, corporation tax or capital gains tax, and all the appropriate conditions of section 75 of the Finance Act 1986 have been complied with, and accordingly exemption from ad valorem stamp duty under the head "Conveyance or Transfer on Sale" is claimed in respect of the Agreement and the transfers executed pursuant thereto.

12.   We enclose for adjudication [describe document] together with [a] certified [copy/copies].

Would you kindly telephone in the first instance M .... should you require any further information.

Yours faithfully

This index is referenced to section and paragraph numbers. The entries in bold capitals are the main subject headings in the text.

Index

Index

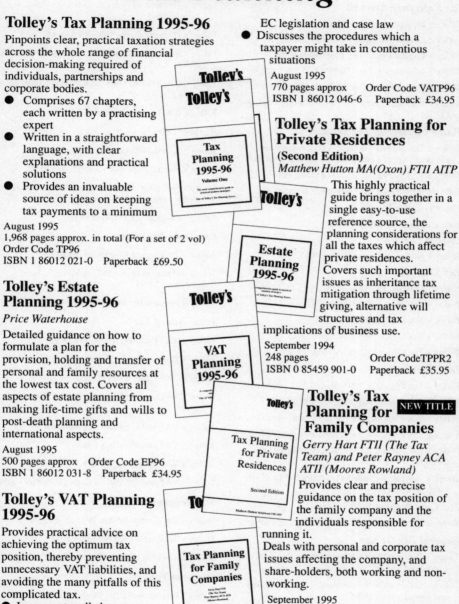

TAXATION PUBLICATIONS

Tax Reference Annuals

Tolley's Income Tax 1995-96 £32.95

Tolley's Corporation Tax 1995-96 £28.95

Tolley's Capital Gains Tax 1995-96 £29.95

Tolley's Inheritance Tax 1995-96 £25.95

Tolley's Value Added Tax 1995-96 £28.95

Tolley's National Insurance Contributions 1995-96 £33.95

Tolley's Looseleaf Tax Services

Tolley's Tax Service (Income Tax, Corporation Tax and Capital Gains Tax) (4 volumes) £450.00

Tolley's VAT Service £325.00 (2 volumes)

Tolley's Inheritance Tax Service £120.00

Tax Periodicals

Tolley's Practical Tax £113 p.a.

Taxation £107 p.a.

Tolley's National Insurance Brief £132 p.a.

Tax Sources

Tolley's Official Tax Statements 1995-96 £39.95

Tolley's Tax Tables 1996-97 £12.95

Tolley's Tax Data 1995-96 £16.95

Tolley's Tax Cases 1995 £32.95

Tolley's Tax Office Directory 1996 £9.95

Tax Planning

Tolley's Tax Planning 1995-96 £69.50 (2 volumes)

Tolley's Estate Planning 1995-96 £34.95

Tolley's Tax Planning for Family Companies £tba

Tolley's Tax Planning for Private Residences £35.95

Tolley's Tax Planning for Post-Death Variations £36.95

Tolley's Adviser's Guide to Investment Planning 1995-96 £tba

Tax Compliance

Tolley's Tax Compliance and Investigations £tba

General Tax Guides

Tolley's Guide to Self-Assessment for the Self-Employed £16.95

Tolley's Guide to Self-Assessment for Employers and Employees £16.95

Tolley's Accounting Principles for Tax Purposes £36.95

Tolley's Self-Assessment £35.95

Tolley's Tax Guide 1995-96 £24.95

Specialist Tax Guides

Tolley's Anti-Avoidance Provisions £52.50

Tolley's Taxation of Lloyds Underwriters £55.00

Tolley's Taxation in Corporate Insolvency £tba

Tolley's Taxation of Foreign Exchange Gains and Losses £49.95

Tolley's Property Taxes 1995-96 £36.95

Tolley's Stamp Duties and Stamp Duty Reserve Tax £29.95

Tolley's Purchase and Sale of a Private Company's Shares £34.95

Tolley's UK Taxation of Trusts £37.95

Business Tax

Tolley's Schedule D £tba

Tolley's Capital Allowances 1995-96 £31.95

Tolley's Roll-over, Hold-over and Retirement Reliefs £39.95

Tolley's Partnership Taxation £tba

Employee Taxation

Tolley's Taxation of Employments £34.95

Tolley's Practical Guide to Employees' Share Schemes £36.95

Tolley's Pay and Benefits Handbook £23.95

Value Added Tax

Tolley's VAT Planning 1995-96 £34.95

Tolley's Practical VAT (Newsletter) £103 p.a.

Tolley's VAT Cases 1995 £60.00

Tolley's VAT on Construction, Land and Property £29.95

Tolley's VAT and Customs Appeals £tba

Tolley's VAT and Retailers £tba

Tolley's VAT in Europe £34.95

Tolley's VAT and the Partial Exemption Rules £tba

Tax Computations

Tolley's Tax Computations 1995-96 £35.95

Tolley's Taxwise I 1995-96 £26.95

Tolley's Taxwise II 1995-96 £25.95

Overseas Tax

Tolley's International Tax Planning £99.50

Tolley's Tax Havens £54.50

Tolley's Taxation of Offshore Trusts and Funds £49.50

Tolley's Taxation in the Republic of Ireland 1995-96 £29.95

Tolley's Taxation in the Channel Islands and Isle of Man 1995-96 £29.95

ORDER FORM

PLEASE PHOTOCOPY AND SEND TO:

Tolley Publishing Company Ltd., FREEPOST, Tolley House, 2 Addiscombe Road, Croydon, Surrey CR9 5WZ
or call our Customer Services Department on 0181-686 9141

Delivery: Thank you for your order – your copy(ies) will be despatched to you from stock or upon publication.

Full Refund Guarantee: If, for any reason, you are not satisfied with your order simply return the goods in saleable condition within 21 days and upon request we will refund your money promptly and in full.

Tolley Tax books
Please list the titles that you require on the form below:

Title	No. of copies	Price	Amount £
		Total £	

SIGNATURE _____ Date _____

Surname _____

Initials _____ Title (Mr, Mrs, Miss, Ms) _____

Job Title _____ Telephone _____

Full Name of Firm *(if applicable)* _____

Address _____

_____

_____ Postcode _____

Type of Organisation/Business _____

Number of Employees A ❑ 1-5 B ❑ 6-50 C ❑ 51-200 D ❑ 201-1000 E ❑ 1000+

Registered No.729731 England   VAT Registered No.243 3583 67

CHOICE OF PAYMENT METHOD:

Cheque enclosed £

_____

Please make cheques payable to:
Tolley Publishing Company Ltd.

Please debit Tolley/Access/Visa† Account No.

_____

† *Please delete as necessary*

Expiry Date

____ / ____
Month   Year

Please enter name and address of cardholder

Name _____

Address _____

_____

_____ Postcode _____

If you have a Tolley Account but have chosen to pay by cheque, Access or Visa please enter your Tolley Account Number to help us process your order

_____

Tolley
A114

Please tick to request further information	
Tolley Catalogue 1995-96	❑
Details of Tolley Conferences	❑
Details of Client Marketing Services	❑

NOTES